PROGRAMMER'S
Q U I C K
REFERENCE
S E R I E S

W9-CXP-717

MS-DOS®
EXTENSIONS

□ □ □ □ □

R A Y   D U N C A N

Microsoft PRESS®

Covers expanded memory, extended memory,
CD-ROM, and the Microsoft®Mouse

PUBLISHED BY
Microsoft Press
A Division of Microsoft Corporation
16011 NE 36th Way, Box 97017, Redmond, Washington 98073-9717

Library of Congress Cataloging in Publication Data

Duncan, Ray, 1952–
MS-DOS extensions : programmer's quick reference / Ray Duncan.
        p.   cm.
Includes index.
1. MS-DOS (Computer operating system)   I. Title.
QA76.76.O63D8588   1989   89-7962
005.4'46--dc20   CIP
ISBN 1-55615-212-4: $6.95

Printed and bound in the United States of America.

1 2 3 4 5 6 7 8 9 WAKWAK 3 2 1 0 9

Distributed to the book trade in the United States by Harper & Row.

Distributed to the book trade in Canada by General Publishing
Company, Ltd.

Distributed to the book trade outside the United States and Canada
by Penguin Books Ltd.

Penguin Books Ltd., Harmondsworth, Middlesex, England
Penguin Books Australia Ltd., Ringwood, Victoria, Australia
Penguin Books N.Z. Ltd., 182-190 Wairau Road, Auckland 10,
New Zealand

British Cataloging in Publication Data available

Project Editor: Jack Litewka
Technical Editor: Jim Johnson

Contents

Microsoft Mouse Driver

The Microsoft Mouse driver offers a comprehensive battery of services to query and control the mouse's position, behavior, and pointer appearance. The driver can also notify an application program of a change in mouse state by calling a handler routine registered by that program. The Microsoft Mouse driver's functionality has become a de facto standard for pointer device drivers of all varieties.

Driver Installation

The Microsoft Mouse driver MOUSE.SYS is loaded at system boot time by a DEVICE= directive in the CONFIG.SYS file. An alternate version of the driver, supplied in the file MOUSE.COM, can be loaded by placing its name in the AUTOEXEC.BAT file or by entering its name at any other convenient time.

Determining Presence of the Driver

An application program can determine whether the Microsoft Mouse driver (or a compatible driver for another type of pointing device) is available by executing an Int 33H with AX = 0. If the driver is present, it returns AX = FFFFH; if the driver is absent, AX is unchanged.

```
                                ; check if driver available
        xor     ax,ax           ; set AX to 0
        int     33h             ; call driver
        or      ax,ax           ; was AX changed?
        jnz     present         ; yes, driver is present
        jmp     absent          ; no, driver is absent
```

Using Driver Functions

Mouse driver functions are called by placing a function number in register AX, loading other registers with function-specific parameters, and executing an Int 33H. Most functions return results in registers, although a few return data in a buffer specified by the calling program.

Reference

The information in this section applies to Microsoft Mouse driver version 6.0 and has been checked against the Microsoft Mouse

Programmer's Reference Guide. Earlier versions of the driver might
not support all of these functions.

Summary of Mouse Functions

Function	Name
00H	Reset Mouse and Get Status
01H	Show Mouse Pointer
02H	Hide Mouse Pointer
03H	Get Mouse Position and Button Status
04H	Set Pointer Position
05H	Get Button Press Information
06H	Get Button Release Information
07H	Set Horizontal Limits for Pointer
08H	Set Vertical Limits for Pointer
09H	Set Graphics Pointer Shape
0AH	Set Text Pointer Type
0BH	Read Mouse Motion Counters
0CH	Set User-defined Mouse Event Handler
0DH	Turn On Light Pen Emulation
0EH	Turn Off Light Pen Emulation
0FH	Set Mickeys to Pixels Ratio
10H	Set Mouse Pointer Exclusion Area
13H	Set Double-Speed Threshold
14H	Swap User-defined Mouse Event Handlers
15H	Get Mouse Save State Buffer Size
16H	Save Mouse Driver State
17H	Restore Mouse Driver State
18H	Set Alternate Mouse Event Handler
19H	Get Address of Alternate Mouse Event Handler
1AH	Set Mouse Sensitivity
1BH	Get Mouse Sensitivity
1CH	Set Mouse Interrupt Rate
1DH	Select Pointer Page
1EH	Get Pointer Page
1FH	Disable Mouse Driver

(continued)

Function	Name
20H	Enable Mouse Driver
21H	Reset Mouse Driver
22H	Set Language for Mouse Driver Messages
23H	Get Language Number
24H	Get Mouse Information

Mouse Function 00H
Reset Mouse and Get Status

Initializes the mouse driver, and returns the driver status. If the mouse pointer was previously visible, it is removed from the screen, and any previously installed user handlers for mouse events are disabled.

Call with:

AX   = 0000H

Returns:

If mouse support is available
AX   = FFFFH
BX   = number of mouse buttons

If mouse support is not available
AX   = 0000H

Note:

■ After a call to this function, the mouse driver is initialized to the following state:

 – Mouse pointer at screen center (see Mouse Functions 03H and 04H);

 – Display page for mouse pointer set to 0 (see Mouse Functions 1DH and 1EH);

 – Mouse pointer hidden (see Mouse Functions 01H, 02H, and 10H);

 – Mouse pointer set to default arrow shape in graphics modes or to reverse block in text modes (see Mouse Functions 09H and 0AH);

 – User mouse event handler disabled (see Mouse Functions 0CH and 14H);

 – Light pen emulation enabled (see Mouse Functions 0DH and 0EH);

3

- Horizontal mickeys to pixels ratio at 8 to 8 and vertical ratio at 16 to 8 (see Mouse Function 0FH);
- Double-speed threshold set to 64 mickeys per second (see Mouse Function 13H);
- Minimum and maximum horizontal and vertical pointer position limits set to include the entire screen in the current display mode (see Mouse Functions 07H and 08H).

Mouse Function 01H
Show Mouse Pointer

Displays the mouse pointer, and cancels any mouse pointer exclusion area previously defined with Mouse Function 10H.

Call with:

AX   = 0001H

Returns:

Nothing

Note:

- A counter is maintained; it is decremented by calls to Mouse Function 02H and incremented (if nonzero) with this function. When the counter is 0 or becomes 0, the mouse pointer is displayed. When the mouse driver is reset with Mouse Function 00H, the counter is forced to −1.

Mouse Function 02H
Hide Mouse Pointer

Removes the mouse pointer from the display. The driver continues to track the mouse position.

Call with:

AX   = 0002H

Returns:

Nothing

Note:

■ A counter is maintained; it is decremented by calls to this function and incremented (if nonzero) by Mouse Function 01H. When the counter is 0 or becomes 0, the mouse pointer is displayed. When the mouse driver is reset with Mouse Function 00H, the counter is forced to −1.

Mouse Function 03H
Get Mouse Position and Button Status

Returns the current mouse button status and pointer position.

Call with:

AX   = 0003H

Returns:

BX   = mouse button status

Bit(s)	*Significance (if set)*
0	*left button is down*
1	*right button is down*
2	*center button is down*
3–15	*reserved (0)*

CX   = horizontal (*x*) coordinate
DX   = vertical (*y*) coordinate

Note:

■ Coordinates are returned in pixels, regardless of the current display mode. Position (*x,y*) = (0,0) is the upper left corner of the screen.

Mouse Function 04H
Set Mouse Pointer Position

Sets the position of the mouse pointer. The pointer is displayed at the new position unless it has been hidden with Mouse Function 02H or unless the new position lies within an exclusion area defined with Mouse Function 10H.

Call with:

AX = 0004H
CX = horizontal (*x*) coordinate
DX = vertical (*y*) coordinate

Returns:

Nothing

Notes:

■ Coordinates are specified in pixels, regardless of the current display mode. Position (*x,y*) = (0,0) is the upper left corner of the screen.

■ The position is adjusted (if necessary) to lie within the horizontal and vertical limits specified with a previous call to Mouse Functions 07H and 08H.

Mouse Function 05H
Get Button Press Information

Returns the current status of all mouse buttons and the number of presses and position of the last press for a specified mouse button since the last call to this function for that button. The press counter for the button is reset to 0.

Call with:

AX = 0005H
BX = button identifier
  0 = left button
  1 = right button
  2 = center button

Returns:

AX = button status

Bit(s)	*Significance (if set)*
0	*left button is down*
1	*right button is down*
2	*center button is down*
3–15	*reserved (0)*

BX = button press counter (0–32,767)
CX = horizontal (*x*) coordinate of last button press
DX = vertical (*y*) coordinate of last button press

Mouse Function 06H
Get Button Release Information

Returns the current status of all mouse buttons and the number of
releases and position of the last release for a specified mouse button
since the last call to this function for that button. The release counter
for the button is reset to 0.

Call with:

AX	= 0006H
BX	= button identifier
	0 = *left button*
	1 = *right button*
	2 = *center button*

Returns:

AX	= button status

Bit(s)	*Significance (if set)*
0	*left button is down*
1	*right button is down*
2	*center button is down*
3–15	*reserved (0)*

BX	= button release counter (0–32,767)
CX	= horizontal (x) coordinate of last button release
DX	= vertical (y) coordinate of last button release

Mouse Function 07H
Set Horizontal Limits for Pointer

Limits the mouse pointer display area by assigning minimum and
maximum horizontal (x) coordinates for the mouse pointer.

Call with:

AX	= 0007H
CX	= minimum horizontal (x) coordinate
DX	= maximum horizontal (x) coordinate

Returns:

Nothing

- If the minimum value is greater than the maximum value, the two values are swapped.

- The mouse pointer will be moved (if necessary) so that it lies within the specified horizontal coordinates.

- See also Mouse Function 10H, which defines an exclusion area for the mouse pointer.

Mouse Function 08H
Set Vertical Limits for Pointer

Limits the mouse pointer display area by assigning minimum and maximum vertical (y) coordinates for the mouse pointer.

Call with:

AX	= 0008H
CX	= minimum vertical (y) coordinate
DX	= maximum vertical (y) coordinate

Returns:

Nothing

Notes:

- If the minimum value is greater than the maximum value, the two values are swapped.

- The mouse pointer will be moved (if necessary) so that it lies within the specified vertical coordinates.

- See also Mouse Function 10H, which defines an exclusion area for the mouse pointer.

Mouse Function 09H
Set Graphics Pointer Shape

Defines the shape, color, and hot spot of the mouse pointer in graphics modes.

Call with:

AX	= 0009H
BX	= hot spot offset from left
CX	= hot spot offset from top
ES:DX	= segment:offset of pointer image buffer

Returns:

Nothing

Notes:

■ The pointer image buffer is 64 bytes long. The first 32 bytes contain a bit mask (which is ANDed with the screen image), and the second 32 bytes contain a bit mask (which is XORed with the screen image).

■ The hot spot is relative to the upper left corner of the pointer image, and each pixel offset must be in the range −16 through 16. In display modes 4 and 5, the horizontal offset must be an even number.

Mouse Function 0AH (10)
Set Text Pointer Type

Defines the shape and attributes of the mouse pointer in text modes.

Call with:

AX	= 000AH
BX	= pointer type
	0 = software cursor
	1 = hardware cursor
CX	= AND mask value (if BX = 0) *or*
	starting line for cursor (if BX = 1)
DX	= XOR mask value (if BX = 0) *or*
	ending line for cursor (if BX = 1)

Returns:

Nothing

Notes:

■ If the software text cursor is selected (BX = 0), the masks in CX and DX are mapped as follows:

Bit(s)	Significance
0–7	Character code
8–10	Foreground color
11	Intensity
12–14	Background color
15	Blink

For example, the following values would yield a software mouse cursor that inverts the foreground and background colors:

AX	= 000AH
BX	= 0000H
CX	= 77FFH
DX	= 7700H

- When the hardware text cursor is selected (BX = 1), the values in CX and DX are the starting and ending scan lines for the blinking cursor generated by the video adapter. The maximum scan line that can be used depends on the type of adapter and the current display mode.

Mouse Function 0BH (11)
Read Mouse Motion Counters

Returns the net mouse displacement since the last call to this function. The returned value is in mickeys: A positive number indicates travel to the right or downward, and a negative number indicates travel to the left or upward. One mickey represents approximately $1/200$ inch of mouse movement. The range of values is –32,768 through 32,767.

Call with:

AX	= 000BH

Returns:

CX	= horizontal (x) mickey count
DX	= vertical (y) mickey count

Mouse Function 0CH (12)
Set User-defined Mouse Event Handler

Sets the address and event mask for an application program's mouse event handler. The handler is called by the mouse driver whenever the specified mouse events occur.

Call with:

AX   = 000CH
CX   = event mask

Bit(s)	*Significance (if set)*
0	*mouse movement*
1	*left button pressed*
2	*left button released*
3	*right button pressed*
4	*right button released*
5	*center button pressed*
6	*center button released*
7–15	*reserved (0)*

ES:DX   = segment:offset of handler

Returns:

Nothing

Notes:

■ The user-defined event handler is entered from the mouse driver by a far call, with registers set up as follows:

AX   mouse event flags (same bit assignments as event mask; see Call with)

BX   button state

Bit(s)	*Significance (if set)*
0	*left button is down*
1	*right button is down*
2	*center button is down*
3–15	*reserved (0)*

CX   horizontal (*x*) pointer coordinate
DX   vertical (*y*) pointer coordinate
SI   last raw vertical mickey count
DI   last raw horizontal mickey count
DS   mouse driver data segment

■ If an event does not generate a call to the user-defined handler because its bit is not set in the event mask, it is still reported in the event flags during calls to the handler for events that *are* enabled.

■ Calls to the handler are disabled with Mouse Function 00H or by calling this function with an event mask of 0.

■ See also Mouse Functions 14H and 18H.

Mouse Function 0DH (13)
Turn On Light Pen Emulation

Enables light pen emulation by the mouse driver for IBM BASIC. A "pen down" condition is created by simultaneously pressing the left and right mouse buttons.

Call with:

AX   = 000DH

Returns:

Nothing

Mouse Function 0EH (14)
Turn Off Light Pen Emulation

Disables light pen emulation by the mouse driver for IBM BASIC.

Call with:

AX   = 000EH

Returns:

Nothing

Mouse Function 0FH (15)
Set Mickeys to Pixels Ratio

Sets the number of mickeys per 8 pixels for horizontal and vertical mouse motion. One mickey represents approximately $1/200$ inch of mouse travel.

Call with:

AX   = 000FH
CX   = horizontal mickeys (1–32,767, default = 8)
DX   = vertical mickeys (1–32,767, default = 16)

Returns:

Nothing

Mouse Function 10H (16)
Set Mouse Pointer Exclusion Area

Defines an exclusion area for the mouse pointer. When the mouse pointer lies within the specified area, it is not displayed.

Call with:

AX	= 0010H
CX	= upper left x coordinate
DX	= upper left y coordinate
SI	= lower right x coordinate
DI	= lower right y coordinate

Returns:

Nothing

Note:

■ The exclusion area is replaced with another call to this function or canceled with Mouse Function 00H or 01H.

Mouse Function 13H (19)
Set Double-Speed Threshold

Sets the threshold speed for doubling pointer motion on the screen. The default threshold speed is 64 mickeys per second.

Call with:

AX	= 0013H
DX	= threshold speed in mickeys/second

Returns:

Nothing

Note:

■ Doubling of pointer motion can be effectively disabled by setting the threshold to a very large value (such as 10,000).

Mouse Function 14H (20)
Swap User-defined Mouse Event Handlers

Sets the address and event mask for an application program's mouse
event handler, and returns the address and event mask for the previous
handler. The newly installed handler is called by the mouse driver
whenever the specified mouse events occur.

Call with:

AX = 0014H
CX = event mask

Bit(s)	Significance (if set)
0	mouse movement
1	left button pressed
2	left button released
3	right button pressed
4	right button released
5	center button pressed
6	center button released
7–15	reserved (0)

ES:DX = segment:offset of event handler

Returns:

CX = previous event mask
ES:DX = segment:offset of previous handler

Notes:

■ The Notes for Mouse Function 0CH describe the information
  passed to the user-defined event handler. See also Mouse Function
  18H.

■ Calls to the event handler are disabled with Mouse Function 00H or
  by setting an event mask of 0.

Mouse Function 15H (21)
Get Mouse Save State Buffer Size

Gets the size of the buffer required to store the current state of the
mouse driver.

AX   = 0015H

Returns:

BX   = buffer size (bytes)

Note:

■ See also Mouse Functions 16H and 17H.

Mouse Function 16H (22)
Save Mouse Driver State

Saves the mouse driver state in a user buffer. The minimum size for the buffer must be determined by a previous call to Mouse Function 15H.

Call with:

AX   = 0016H
ES:DX   = segment:offset of buffer

Returns:

Nothing

Note:

■ Call this function before executing another program with Int 21H Function 4BH (EXEC), in case that other program also uses the mouse. After the EXEC call, restore the previous mouse driver state with Mouse Function 17H.

Mouse Function 17H (23)
Restore Mouse Driver State

Restores the mouse driver state from a user buffer.

Call with:

AX   = 0017H
ES:DX   = segment:offset of buffer

Returns:

Nothing

■ The mouse driver state must have been previously saved in the same buffer with Mouse Function 16H. The format of the data in the buffer is undocumented and subject to change.

Mouse Function 18H (24)
Set Alternate Mouse Event Handler

Sets the address and event mask for an application program mouse event handler. This function can register as many as three handlers with distinct event masks. When an event occurs that matches one of the masks, the corresponding handler is called by the mouse driver.

Call with:

AX   = 0018H
CX   = event mask

Bit(s)	*Significance (if set)*
0	*mouse movement*
1	*left button pressed*
2	*left button released*
3	*right button pressed*
4	*right button released*
5	*Shift key pressed during button press or release*
6	*Ctrl key pressed during button press or release*
7	*Alt key pressed during button press or release*
8–15	*reserved (0)*

ES:DX   = segment:offset of handler

Returns:

If function successful
AX   = 0018H

If function unsuccessful
AX   = FFFFH

Notes:

■ When this function is called, at least one of the bits 5, 6, or 7 must be set in register CX.

■ The user-defined event handler is entered from the mouse driver by a far call, with registers set up as follows:

AX   mouse event flags (same bit assignments as event mask; see Call with)

BX   button state

Bit(s)	*Significance (if set)*
0	*left button is down*
1	*right button is down*
2	*center button is down*
3–15	*reserved (0)*

CX   horizontal (*x*) pointer coordinate

DX   vertical (*y*) pointer coordinate

SI   last raw vertical mickey count

DI   last raw horizontal mickey count

DS   mouse driver data segment

■ If an event does not generate a call to the user-defined handler because its bit is not set in the event mask, it can still be reported in the event flags during calls to the handler for events that *are* enabled.

■ Calls to the handler are disabled with Mouse Function 00H.

■ See also Mouse Functions 0CH, 14H, and 19H.

Mouse Function 19H (25)
Get Address of Alternate Mouse Event Handler

Returns the address for the mouse event handler matching the specified event mask.

Call with:

AX   = 0019H

CX   = event mask (see Mouse Function 18H)

Returns:

If function successful

CX   = event mask

ES:DX   = segment:offset of alternate event handler

If function unsuccessful (no handler installed, or event mask does not match any installed handler)

CX   = 0000H

■ Mouse Function 18H allows installation of as many as three event handlers with distinct event masks. This function can be called to search for a handler that matches a specific event so that it can be replaced or disabled.

Mouse Function 1AH (26)
Set Mouse Sensitivity

Sets the number of mickeys per 8 pixels for horizontal and vertical mouse motion and the threshold speed for doubling pointer motion on the screen. One mickey represents approximately $1/200$ inch of mouse travel.

Call with:

AX	= 001AH
BX	= horizontal mickeys (1–32,767, default = 8)
CX	= vertical mickeys (1–32,767, default = 16)
DX	= double-speed threshhold in mickeys/second (default = 64)

Returns:

Nothing

Note:

■ See also Mouse Functions 0FH and 13H (which allow the mickeys to pixels ratio and threshold speed to be set separately) and Mouse Function 1BH (which returns the current sensitivity values).

Mouse Function 1BH (27)
Get Mouse Sensitivity

Returns the current mickeys to pixels ratios for vertical and horizontal screen movement and the threshold speed for doubling of pointer motion.

Call with:

AX	= 001BH

Returns:

BX   = horizontal mickeys (1–32,767, default = 8)
CX   = vertical mickeys (1–32,767, default = 16)
DX   = double-speed threshhold in mickeys/second
           (default = 64)

Note:

■ See also Mouse Functions 0FH, 13H, and 1AH.

Mouse Function 1CH (28)
Set Mouse Interrupt Rate

Sets the rate at which the mouse driver polls the status of the mouse. Faster rates provide better resolution in graphics mode but can degrade the performance of application programs.

Call with:

AX   = 001CH
BX   = interrupt rate flags

Bit(s)	*Significance (if set)*
0	*no interrupts allowed*
1	*30 interrupts/second*
2	*50 interrupts/second*
3	*100 interrupts/second*
4	*200 interrupts/second*
5–15	*reserved (0)*

Returns:

Nothing

Notes:

■ This function is applicable for the InPort Mouse only.

■ If more than one bit is set in register BX, the lowest-order bit prevails.

Mouse Function 1DH (29)
Select Pointer Page

Selects the display page for the mouse pointer.

Call with:

AX   = 001DH
BX   = page

Returns:

Nothing

Note:

■ The valid page numbers depend on the current display mode.

Mouse Function 1EH (30)
Get Pointer Page

Returns the current display page for the mouse pointer.

Call with:

AX   = 001EH

Returns:

BX   = page

Note:

■ The valid page numbers depend on the current display mode.

Mouse Function 1FH (31)
Disable Mouse Driver

Disables the mouse driver, and returns the address of the previous Int 33H handler.

Call with:

AX   = 001FH

Returns:

If function successful
AX   = 001FH
ES:BX   = segment:offset of previous Int 33H handler

If function unsuccessful
AX   = FFFFH

Notes:

■ When this function is called, the mouse driver releases any interrupt vectors it has captured *other* than Int 33H (which can include
Int 10H, Int 71H, and/or Int 74H). The application program can
complete the process of logically removing the mouse driver by
restoring the original contents of the Int 33H vector with Int 21H
Function 25H, using the address returned by this function in
ES:BX.

■ See also Mouse Function 20H.

Mouse Function 20H (32)
Enable Mouse Driver

Enables the mouse driver and the servicing of mouse interrupts.

Call with:

AX   = 0020H

Returns:

Nothing

Note:

■ See also Mouse Function 1FH.

Mouse Function 21H (33)
Reset Mouse Driver

Resets the mouse driver and returns driver status. If the mouse pointer
was previously visible, it is removed from the screen, and any previously installed user handlers for mouse events are disabled.

Call with:

AX   = 0021H

Returns:

If mouse support is available
AX   = FFFFH
BX   = number of mouse buttons

If mouse support is not available
AX   = 0021H

<u>Note:</u>

■ This function differs from Mouse Function 00H because initialization of the mouse hardware does not occur.

Mouse Function 22H (34)
Set Language for Mouse Driver Messages

Selects the language that will be used by the mouse driver for prompts and error messages.

<u>Call with:</u>

AX   = 0022H
BX   = language number
    0 = English
    1 = French
    2 = Dutch
    3 = German
    4 = Swedish
    5 = Finnish
    6 = Spanish
    7 = Portuguese
    8 = Italian

<u>Returns:</u>

Nothing

<u>Notes:</u>

■ This function is available only in the international versions of the Microsoft Mouse driver.

■ See also Mouse Function 23H.

Mouse Function 23H (35)
Get Language Number

Returns the number of the language that is used by the mouse driver for prompts and error messages.

Call with:

AX   = 0023H

Returns:

BX   = language number (see Mouse Function 22H)

Notes:

■ This function is available only in the international versions of the Microsoft Mouse driver.

■ See also Mouse Function 23H.

Mouse Function 24H (36)
Get Mouse Information

Returns the mouse driver version number, mouse type, and the IRQ number of the interrupt used by the mouse adapter.

Call with:

AX   = 0024H

Returns:

BH   = major version number (6 for version 6.10, etc.)
BL   = minor version number (0AH for version 6.10, etc.)
CH   = mouse type
    1 = bus mouse
    2 = serial mouse
    3 = InPort mouse
    4 = PS/2 mouse
    5 = HP mouse
CL   = IRQ number
    0 = PS/2
    2, 3, 4, 5, or 7 = IRQ number

Lotus/Intel/Microsoft Expanded Memory Specification (EMS)

The Lotus/Intel/Microsoft Expanded Memory Specification (EMS) defines a hardware/software subsystem, compatible with 80x86-based microcomputers running MS-DOS, that allows applications to access as much as 32 MB of bank-switched random-access memory.

An icon in each EMS function heading indicates the EMS version in which that function was first supported. You can assume that the function is available in all subsequent EMS versions unless explicitly noted otherwise.

Driver Installation

The software component of an expanded memory subsystem, called the Expanded Memory Manager (EMM), is installed during system initialization by a DEVICE= directive in the CONFIG.SYS file on the boot disk. The filename of the driver varies from one manufacturer to another, but the logical device name in the EMM's device driver header is always EMMXXXX0.

Determining Presence of Driver

An application program can use two basic methods to establish the presence or absence of the EMM. Both methods rely on the fact that the EMM masquerades as a character device driver, to the extent that it has a valid device driver header and supports the driver initialization and input status functions.

The first technique requires that the application open the driver by its logical device name, then use Int 21H Function 44H (IOCTL) to ensure that a file with the same name has not been opened by accident.

```
        .
        .
                            ; attempt to open EMM...
        mov     dx,seg emmname   ; DS:DX = address of EMM
        mov     ds,dx            ; logical device name
        mov     dx,offset emmname
        mov     ax,3d00h         ; Function 3DH, read-only access
```

(continued)

```
        int     21h             ; transfer to MS-DOS
        jc      error           ; jump if open failed

                                ; open succeeded, make sure
                                ; it was not a file...
        mov     bx,ax           ; BX = handle from open
        mov     ax,4400h        ; Function 44H Subfunction 00H =
                                ; IOCTL get device info.
        int     21h             ; transfer to MS-DOS
        jc      error           ; jump if IOCTL call failed
        and     dx,80h          ; bit 7 = 1 if character device
        jz      error           ; jump if it was a file

                                ; EMM is present, make sure
                                ; it is available...
                                ; (BX still contains handle)
        mov     ax,4407h        ; Function 44H Subfunction 07H =
                                ; IOCTL get output status
        int     21h             ; transfer to MS-DOS
        jc      error           ; jump if IOCTL call failed
        or      al,al           ; test device status
        jz      error           ; if AL=0 EMM not available

                                ; now close handle...
                                ; (BX still contains handle)
        mov     ah,3eh          ; Function 3EH = close
        int     21h             ; transfer to MS-DOS
        jc      error           ; jump if close failed
        .
        .


emmname db      'EMMXXXX0',0    ; guaranteed device name for
                                ; Expanded Memory Manager
```

The second technique for establishing the presence of an EMM
assumes that the interrupt vector for Int 67H points to the EMM's
device driver header. The program can then compare the name field of
the header, which is always located at offset 0AH, with the expected
EMM logical device name.

```
emmint  equ     67h             ; Extended Memory Manager
                                ; software interrupt
        .
        .
        .
                                ; first fetch contents of
                                ; EMM interrupt vector...
        mov     al,emmint       ; AL = EMM Int number
```

```
        mov     ah,35h          ; Function 35H = get vector
        int     21h             ; transfer to MS-DOS
                                ; now ES:BX = handler address

                                ; assume ES:0000 points
                                ; to base of the EMM...
        mov     di,10           ; ES:DI = address of name
                                ; field in Device Header
        mov     si,seg emmname  ; DS:SI = EMM driver name
        mov     ds,si
        mov     si,offset emmname
        mov     cx,8            ; length of name field
        cld
        repz    cmpsb           ; compare names...
        jnz     error           ; jump if driver absent
        .
        .
        .


emmname db      'EMMXXXX0'      ; guaranteed device name for
                                ; Expanded Memory Manager
```

Device drivers that use expanded memory must use a variation on the
second technique, fetching the contents of the Int 67H vector directly.
This is because the MS-DOS Int 21H Functions 35H (Get Interrupt
Vector), 3DH (Open File or Device), and 44H (IOCTL) cannot be
called by device drivers.

Using Driver Functions

After establishing that the EMM is present, an application program or
driver communicates with it directly via Int 67H, bypassing MS-DOS.
A particular EMM function is selected by the value in register AH.
Other parameters are passed in registers or structures. For example,
register BX is often used to hold a number of EMM pages, register DX
typically contains an EMM handle for an allocated memory block,
and registers DS:SI or ES:DI can point to an array or buffer.

```
        mov     ah,function     ; AH selects EMM function
        .                       ; load other registers
        .                       ; with function-specific
        .                       ; values...
        int     67h             ; transfer to EMM
```

Upon return from an EMM function call, register AH contains 0 if the
function was successful or an error code with the most significant bit
set if the function failed. Other results are usually returned in registers
AL or BX or in a user-specified buffer.

Reference

The material in this section has been checked against the Expanded Memory Specification version 4.0, dated October 1987. This document can be obtained from Intel Corporation, 5200 N.E. Elam Young Parkway, Hillsboro, OR 97124.

EMS Error Codes

If an error occurs during execution of an EMS function, the driver returns bit 7 of AH = 1. In that case, the contents of AH are interpreted as follows:

Error code	*Description*
80H	Internal error exists in EMM software (can indicate corrupted memory image of driver)
81H	Malfunction exists in expanded memory hardware
82H	EMM is busy
83H	Handle is invalid
84H	Function is not defined
85H	Handles are exhausted
86H	Error exists in save or restore of mapping context
87H	Allocation request specified more pages than are physically available in system; no pages were allocated
88H	Allocation request specified more pages than are currently available; no pages were allocated
89H	0 pages cannot be allocated
8AH	Requested logical page is outside range of pages owned by handle
8BH	Illegal physical page number exists in mapping request
8CH	Page-mapping hardware-state save area is full
8DH	Mapping-context save failed; save area already contains context associated with specified handle
8EH	Mapping-context restore failed; save area does not contain context for specified handle
8FH	Subfunction parameter is not defined
90H	Attribute type is not defined
91H	Feature is not supported

(continued)

Error code	Description
92H	Source and destination memory regions have same handle and overlap; requested move was performed, but part of the source region was overwritten
93H	Specified length for source or destination memory region is longer than actual allocated length
94H	Conventional memory region and expanded memory region overlap
95H	Specified offset is outside logical page
96H	Region length exceeds 1 MB
97H	Source and destination memory regions have same handle and overlap; exchange cannot be performed
98H	Memory source and destination types are undefined
99H	Error code is currently unused
9AH	Alternate map or DMA register sets are supported, but specified alternate register set is not supported
9BH	Alternate map or DMA register sets are supported, but all alternate register sets are currently allocated
9CH	Alternate map or DMA register sets are not supported, and specified alternate register set is not 0
9DH	Alternate map or DMA register sets are supported, but the alternate register set specified is not defined or not allocated
9EH	Dedicated DMA channels are not supported
9FH	Dedicated DMA channels are supported, but specified DMA channel is not supported
A0H	Handle for specified name is not found
A1H	Handle with same name already exists
A2H	Memory address wraps; sum of source or destination region base address and length exceeds 1 MB
A3H	Invalid pointer is passed to function, or contents of source array are corrupted
A4H	Access to function is denied by operating system

Summary of EMM Functions

Function	Subfunction	Name
40H		Get Status
41H		Get Page Frame Address
42H		Get Number of Pages
43H		Allocate Handle and Pages
44H		Map Expanded Memory Page
45H		Release Handle and Expanded Memory
46H		Get Version
47H		Save Page Map
48H		Restore Page Map
49H		Reserved
4AH		Reserved
4BH		Get Handle Count
4CH		Get Handle Pages
4DH		Get Pages for All Handles
4EH	00H	Save Page Map
4EH	01H	Restore Page Map
4EH	02H	Save and Restore Page Map
4EH	03H	Get Size of Page-Map Information
4FH	00H	Save Partial Page Map
4FH	01H	Restore Partial Page Map
4FH	02H	Get Size of Partial Page-Map Information
50H	00H	Map Multiple Pages by Number
50H	01H	Map Multiple Pages by Address
51H		Reallocate Pages for Handle
52H	00H	Get Handle Attribute
52H	01H	Set Handle Attribute
52H	02H	Get Attribute Capability
53H	00H	Get Handle Name
53H	01H	Set Handle Name
54H	00H	Get All Handle Names
54H	01H	Search for Handle Name
54H	02H	Get Total Handles

(continued)

Func-tion	Sub-function	Name
55H	00H and 01H	Map Pages and Jump
56H	00H and 01H	Map Pages and Call
56H	02H	Get Stack Space for Map Page and Call
57H	00H	Move Memory Region
57H	01H	Exchange Memory Regions
58H	00H	Get Addresses of Mappable Pages
58H	01H	Get Number of Mappable Pages
59H	00H	Get Hardware Configuration
59H	01H	Get Number of Raw Pages
5AH	00H	Allocate Handle and Standard Pages
5AH	01H	Allocate Handle and Raw Pages
5BH	00H	Get Alternate Map Registers
5BH	01H	Set Alternate Map Registers
5BH	02H	Get Size of Alternate Map Register Save Area
5BH	03H	Allocate Alternate Map Register Set
5BH	04H	Deallocate Alternate Map Register Set
5BH	05H	Allocate DMA Register Set
5BH	06H	Enable DMA on Alternate Map Register Set
5BH	07H	Disable DMA on Alternate Map Register Set
5BH	08H	Deallocate DMA Register Set
5CH		Prepare EMM for Warm Boot
5DH	00H	Enable EMM Operating-System Functions
5DH	01H	Disable EMM Operating-System Functions
5DH	02H	Release Access Key

EMS Function 40H (64)   [3.0]
Get Status

Returns a status code indicating whether the EMM software and hardware are present and functional.

Call with:

AH   = 40H

Returns:

> *If function successful*
> AH   = 00H
>
> *If function unsuccessful*
> AH   = error code

Note:

■ This call should only be used after an application has established
that the EMM is in fact present, using one of the techniques described earlier in this section in "Determining Presence of
Driver."

EMS Function 41H (65)   [3.0]
Get Page Frame Address

Returns the segment address of the page frame used by the EMM.

Call with:

> AH   = 41H

Returns:

> *If function successful*
> AH   = 00H
> BX   = segment base of page frame
>
> *If function unsuccessful*
> AH   = error code

Notes:

■ The page frame is divided into four 16 KB pages that are used to
map logical EMM pages into the physical memory space of the
CPU.

■ The application need not have already acquired an EMM handle to
use this function.

■ [EMS 4] Mapping of EMM pages is not necessarily limited to the
64 KB page frame. See also EMS Function 58H Subfunction 00H.

EMS Function 42H (66)   [3.0]
Get Number of Pages

Obtains the total number of logical EMM pages present in the system
and the number of pages that are not already allocated.

Call with:

AH	= 42H

Returns:

If function successful

AH	= 00H
BX	= unallocated pages
DX	= total pages

If function unsuccessful

AH	= error code

Notes:

- The application need not have already acquired an EMM handle to
  use this function.

- [EMS 4] See also EMS Function 59H Subfunction 01H.

EMS Function 43H (67)   [3.0]
Allocate Handle and Pages

Obtains an EMM handle, and allocates logical EMM pages to be
controlled by that handle.

Call with:

AH	= 43H
BX	= number of pages to allocate (must be nonzero)

Returns:

If function successful

AH	= 00H
DX	= EMM handle

If function unsuccessful

AH	= error code

Notes:

■ This is the equivalent of a file open function for the EMM. The handle that is returned is analogous to a file handle and owns a certain number of EMM pages. The handle must be used with every subsequent request to map memory and must be released by a close operation before the application terminates.

■ This function can fail because no handles are left to allocate or because an insufficient number of EMM pages are available to satisfy the request. In the latter case, EMS Function 42H can be used to determine the actual number of pages available.

■ [EMS 4] EMS Function 51H can be called to change the number of pages allocated to an EMM handle.

■ [EMS 4] The size of pages allocated by this function is 16 KB (for compatibility with earlier versions of EMS). See also EMS Function 5AH Subfunctions 00H and 01H.

■ [EMS 4] Handle 0000H is available for use by the operating system, and a prior call to this function is not required. The operating system must call EMS Function 51H to assign the desired number of pages to its reserved handle.

EMS Function 44H (68)   [3.0]
Map Expanded Memory Page

Maps one of the logical EMM pages assigned to a handle onto a physical memory page that can be accessed by the CPU.

Call with:

AH	= 44H
AL	= physical page
BX	= logical page
DX	= EMM handle

Returns:

If function successful
AH   = 00H

If function unsuccessful
AH   = error code

- The logical page number is in the range $\{0 \ldots n-1\}$, where n is the number of pages allocated or reallocated to the handle by a previous call to EMS Function 43H, 51H, or 5AH. Logical pages allocated by EMS Function 43H or Function 5AH Subfunction 00H are 16 KB long; logical pages allocated by EMS Function 5AH Subfunction 01H are referred to as raw pages and are not necessarily 16 KB.

- [EMS 3] The physical page is in the range 0–3 and lies within the EMM page frame, whose base address is obtained from EMS Function 41H.

- [EMS 4] A list of the available physical pages and their addresses can be obtained from EMS Function 58H Subfunction 00H.

- [EMS 4] If this function is called with BX = −1, the specified physical page is unmapped (made inaccessible for reading or writing).

EMS Function 45H (69)   [3.0]
Release Handle and Expanded Memory

Deallocates the EMM pages assigned to a handle and then releases the handle.

Call with:

AH   = 45H
DX   = EMM handle

Returns:

If function successful
AH   = 00H

If function unsuccessful
AH   = error code

Notes:

- If this function is not called before a program terminates, the EMS pages it owned remain unavailable until the system is restarted. Programs that use EMS should install their own Ctrl-C handlers and critical-error handlers (Ints 23H and 24H) so that they cannot be terminated unexpectedly.

- [EMS 4] When a handle is released, its name is set to all ASCII nulls.

EMS Function 46H (70) [3.0]
Get Version

Returns the EMS version supported by the EMM.

Call with:

AH   = 46H

Returns:

If function successful
AH   = 00H
AL   = version number

If function unsuccessful
AH   = error code

Notes:

■ The version number is returned in binary-coded decimal (BCD)
format, with the integer portion in the upper four bits of AL and the
fractional portion in the lower four bits. For example, under an
EMM that supports EMS 3.2, AL is returned as the value 32H.

■ Applications should always check the EMM version number to
ensure that all of the EMM functions they require are available.

EMS Function 47H (71) [3.0]
Save Page Map

Saves the contents of the page-mapping registers on the expanded
memory hardware, associating those contents with a particular
EMM handle.

Call with:

AH   = 47H
DX   = EMM handle

Returns:

If function successful
AH   = 00H

If function unsuccessful
AH   = error code

Notes:

■ This function is used by interrupt handlers or device drivers that must access expanded memory. The EMM handle supplied to this function is the handle that was assigned to the handler or driver during its own initialization sequence, *not* to the program that was interrupted.

■ The mapping context is restored by a subsequent call to EMS Function 48H.

■ [EMS 4] This function saves only the mapping state for the 64 KB page frame defined in EMS 3. Programs that are written to take advantage of the additional capabilities of EMS 4 should use EMS Function 4EH or 4FH in preference to this function.

EMS Function 48H (72) [3.0]
Restore Page Map

Restores the contents of the page-mapping registers on the expanded memory hardware to the values associated with the specified handle by a previous call to EMS Function 47H.

Call with:

```
AH      = 48H
DX      = EMM handle
```

Returns:

If function successful
```
AH      = 00H
```
If function unsuccessful
```
AH      = error code
```

Notes:

■ This function is used by interrupt handlers or device drivers that must access expanded memory. The EMM handle supplied to this function is the handle that was assigned to the handler or driver during its own initialization sequence, *not* to the program that was interrupted.

■ [EMS 4] This function restores only the mapping state for the 64 KB page frame defined in EMS 3. Programs that are written to take advantage of the additional capabilities of EMS 4 should use EMS Function 4EH or 4FH in preference to this function.

EMS Function 49H (73) [3.0]
Reserved

This function was defined in EMS 3 but is not documented for later
EMS versions, so it should be avoided by application programs.

EMS Function 4AH (74) [3.0]
Reserved

This function was defined in EMS 3 but is not documented for later
EMS versions, so it should be avoided by application programs.

EMS Function 4BH (75) [3.0]
Get Handle Count

Returns the number of active EMM handles.

Call with:

AH   = 4BH

Returns:

If function successful
AH   = 00H
BX   = number of active EMM handles

If function unsuccessful
AH   = error code

Notes:

- If the returned number of EMM handles is 0, the EMM is idle and
  none of the expanded memory is in use.

- The value returned by this function is not necessarily the same as
  the number of programs using expanded memory, because one program can own multiple EMM handles.

- The number of active EMM handles never exceeds 255.

EMS Function 4CH (76) [3.0]
Get Handle Pages

Returns the number of EMM pages allocated to a specific EMM handle.

Call with:

> AH   = 4CH
> DX   = EMM handle

Returns:

> *If function successful*
> AH   = 00H
> BX   = number of EMM pages
>
> *If function unsuccessful*
> AH   = error code

Notes:

- [EMS 3] The total number of pages allocated to a handle never exceeds 512. A handle never has 0 pages allocated to it.

- [EMS 4] The total number of pages allocated to a handle never exceeds 2048. A handle can have 0 pages of expanded memory.

EMS Function 4DH (77) [3.0]
Get Pages for All Handles

Returns an array that contains all the active handles and the number of EMM pages associated with each handle.

Call with:

> AH   = 4DH
> ES:DI = segment:offset of buffer (see Notes)

Returns:

> *If function successful*
> AH   = 00H
> BX   = number of active EMM handles
>
> *and* buffer filled in as described in Notes
>
> *If function unsuccessful*
> AH   = error code

Notes:

■ The buffer is filled in with a series of DWORD (32-bit) entries, one per active EMM handle. The first word of an entry contains the handle, and the second word contains the number of pages allocated to that handle.

■ The maximum number of active handles is 256 (including the operating-system handle 0), so a buffer size of 1024 bytes is adequate in all cases.

EMS Function 4EH (78)   [3.2]
Subfunction 00H
Save Page Map

Saves the current page-mapping state of the expanded memory hardware in the specified buffer.

Call with:

AH	= 4EH
AL	= 00H
ES:DI	= segment:offset of buffer (see Notes)

Returns:

If function successful
AH   = 00H

and buffer filled in with mapping information (see Notes)

If function unsuccessful
AH   = error code

Notes:

■ The buffer receives the information necessary to restore the state of the mapping registers using EMS Function 4EH Subfunction 01H. The format of the information can vary.

■ The size of the buffer required by this function can be determined with EMS Function 4EH Subfunction 03H.

■ Unlike EMS Function 47H, this function does not require a handle.

EMS Function 4EH (78)
Subfunction 01H
Restore Page Map

[3.2]

Restore the page-mapping state of the expanded memory hardware
using the information in the specified buffer.

Call with:

AH	= 4EH
AL	= 01H
DS:SI	= segment:offset of buffer (see Notes)

Returns:

If function successful
AH   = 00H

If function unsuccessful
AH   = error code

Notes:

■ The buffer contains information necessary to restore the state of the
mapping registers from a previous call to EMS Function 4EH Subfunction 00H or 02H. The format of the information can vary.

■ Unlike EMS Function 48H, this function does not require a handle.

EMS Function 4EH (78)
Subfunction 02H
Save and Restore Page Map

[3.2]

Saves the current page-mapping state of the expanded memory hardware in a buffer and then sets the mapping state using the information
in another buffer.

Call with:

AH	= 4EH
AL	= 02H
DS:SI	= segment:offset of buffer containing mapping infor- mation (see Notes)
ES:DI	= segment:offset of buffer to receive mapping infor- mation (see Notes)

Returns:

If function successful
AH   = 00H

and buffer pointed to by ES:DI filled in with mapping information
(see Notes)

If function unsuccessful
AH   = error code

Notes:

- The buffer addressed by DS:SI contains information necessary to
  restore the state of the mapping registers from a previous call to
  EMS Function 4EH Subfunction 00H or 02H. The format of the information can vary.

- The size of the buffers required by this function can be determined
  with EMS Function 4EH Subfunction 03H.

- Unlike EMS Functions 47H and 48H, this function does not require
  a handle.

EMS Function 4EH (78)   [3.2]
Subfunction 03H
Get Size of Page-Map Information

Returns the size of the buffer that is required to receive page-mapping
information using EMS Function 4EH Subfunctions 00H and 02H.

Call with:

AH   = 4EH
AL   = 03H

Returns:

If function successful
AH   = 00H
AL   = size of buffer (bytes)

If function unsuccessful
AH   = error code

EMS Function 4FH (79)   [4.0]
Subfunction 00H
Save Partial Page Map

Saves the state of a subset of the EMM page-mapping registers in the specified buffer.

Call with:

AH	= 4FH
AL	= 00H
DS:SI	= segment:offset of map list (see Notes)
ES:DI	= segment:offset of buffer to receive mapping state (see Notes)

Returns:

If function successful
AH   = 00H

and buffer filled in with mapping information (see Notes)

If function unsuccessful
AH   = error code

Notes:

- The map list contains the number of mappable segments in the first word, followed by the segment addresses of the mappable memory regions (one segment per word).

- To determine the size of the buffer required for the mapping state, use EMS Function 4FH Subfunction 02H.

EMS Function 4FH (79)   [4.0]
Subfunction 01H
Restore Partial Page Map

Restores the state of a subset of the EMM page-mapping registers.

Call with:

AH	= 4FH
AL	= 01H
DS:SI	= segment:offset of buffer (see Note)

Returns:

If function successful
AH   = 00H

If function unsuccessful
AH   = error code

Note:

■ The buffer contains mapping information and must have been prepared by a previous call to EMS Function 4FH Subfunction 00H.

EMS Function 4FH (79)   [4.0]
Subfunction 02H
Get Size of Partial Page-Map Information

Returns the size of the buffer that will be required to receive partial page-mapping information using EMS Function 4FH Subfunction 00H.

Call with:

AH   = 4FH
AL   = 02H
BX   = number of pages

Returns:

If function successful
AH   = 00H
AL   = size of array (bytes)

If function unsuccessful
AH   = error code

EMS Function 50H (50)   [4.0]
Subfunction 00H
Map Multiple Pages by Number

Maps one or more of the logical EMM pages assigned to a handle onto physical memory pages that can be accessed by the CPU. Physical pages are referenced by their numbers.

Call with:

AH	= 50H
AL	= 00H
CX	= number of pages to map
DX	= EMM handle
DS:SI	= segment:offset of buffer (see Note)

Returns:

If function successful
AH   = 00H

If function unsuccessful
AH   = error code

Note:

- The buffer contains a series of DWORD (32-bit) entries that controls the pages to be mapped. The first word of each entry contains the logical EMM page number, and the second word contains the physical page number to which it should be mapped. If the logical page is −1, the physical page is unmapped (made inaccessible for reading or writing).

EMS Function 50H (50)   [4.0]
Subfunction 01H
Map Multiple Pages by Address

Maps one or more of the logical EMM pages assigned to a handle onto physical memory pages that can be accessed by the CPU. Physical pages are referenced by their segment addresses.

Call with:

AH	= 50H
AL	= 01H
CX	= number of pages to map
DX	= EMM handle
DS:SI	= segment:offset of buffer (see Notes)

Returns:

If function successful
AH   = 00H

If function unsuccessful
AH   = error code

Notes:

■ The buffer contains a series of DWORD (32-bit) entries that controls the pages to be mapped. The first word of each entry contains the logical EMM page number, and the second word contains the physical page segment address to which it should be mapped. If the logical page is −1, the physical page is unmapped (made inaccessible for reading or writing).

■ The mappable segment addresses can be obtained by calling EMS Function 58H Subfunction 00H.

EMS Function 51H (81)
Reallocate Pages for Handle

[4.0]

Modifies the number of expanded memory pages allocated to an EMM handle.

Call with:

AH	= 51H
BX	= new number of pages
DX	= EMM handle

Returns:

If function successful

AH	= 00H
BX	= number of logical pages owned by EMM handle

If function unsuccessful

AH	= error code

Note:

■ If the requested number of pages is 0, the handle is still active and pages can be reallocated to the handle at a later time; also, the handle must still be released with EMS Function 45H before the application terminates.

EMS Function 52H (82) [4.0]
Subfunction 00H
Get Handle Attribute

Returns the attribute (volatile or nonvolatile) associated with the
specified handle. A nonvolatile EMM handle and the contents of the
EMM pages that are allocated to it are maintained across a warm boot
operation (system restart using Ctrl-Alt-Del).

Call with:

```
AH      = 52H
AL      = 00H
DX      = EMM handle
```

Returns:

If function successful
```
AH      = 00H
AL      = attribute
            00H = volatile
            01H = nonvolatile
```

If function unsuccessful
```
AH      = error code
```

EMS Function 52H (82) [4.0]
Subfunction 01H
Set Handle Attribute

Sets the attribute (volatile or nonvolatile) associated with the specified
handle. A nonvolatile EMM handle and the contents of the EMM
pages that are allocated to it are maintained across a warm boot operation (system restart using Ctrl-Alt-Del).

Call with:

```
AH       = 52H
AL       = 01H
BL       = attribute
             00H = volatile
             01H = nonvolatile
DX       = EMM handle
```

Returns:

If function successful
AH   = 00H

If function unsuccessful
AH   = error code

Note:

■ EMS Function 52H Subfunction 02H can be used to determine if
the expanded memory hardware can support nonvolatile pages.

EMS Function 52H (82)   [4.0]
Subfunction 02H
Get Attribute Capability

Returns a code indicating whether the EMM and hardware can support the nonvolatile attribute for EMM handles.

Call with:

AH   = 52H
AL   = 02H

Returns:

If function successful
AH   = 00H
AL   = attribute capability
      00H = only volatile handles supported
      01H = volatile and nonvolatile handles supported

If function unsuccessful
AH   = error code

EMS Function 53H (83)   [4.0]
Subfunction 00H
Get Handle Name

Returns the 8-character name assigned to a handle.

Call with:

AH	= 53H
AL	= 00H
DX	= EMM handle
ES:DI	= segment:offset of 8-byte buffer

Returns:

If function successful
AH   = 00H

and name for handle in specified buffer

If function unsuccessful
AH   = error code

Note:

■ A handle's name is initialized to 8 bytes of binary 0 when it is allocated or deallocated. Another name can be assigned to an active handle with EMS Function 53H Subfunction 01H. The bytes in a handle name need not be ASCII characters.

EMS Function 53H (83) [4.0]
Subfunction 01H
Set Handle Name

Assigns a name to an EMM handle.

Call with:

AH	= 53H
AL	= 01H
DX	= handle
DS:SI	= segment:offset of 8-byte name

Returns:

If function successful
AH   = 00H

If function unsuccessful
AH   = error code

Notes:

■ The bytes in a handle name need not be ASCII characters, but the sequence of 8 bytes of binary 0 is reserved for no name (the default after a handle is allocated or deallocated). A handle name should be padded with bytes of binary 0 if necessary to a length of 8 bytes.

■ A handle can be renamed at any time.

■ All handle names are initialized to 8 bytes of binary 0 when the system is turned on. The name of a nonvolatile handle will be preserved across a warm boot. (See EMS Function 52H Subfunctions 00H and 02H.)

EMS Function 54H (84)   [4.0]
Subfunction 00H
Get All Handle Names

Returns the names for all active EMM handles.

Call with:

AH	= 54H
AL	= 00H
ES:DI	= segment:offset of buffer (see Notes)

Returns:

If function successful

AH	= 00H
AL	= number of active handles

and buffer filled in with handle name information (see Notes)

If function unsuccessful

AH	= error code

Notes:

■ The function fills the buffer with a series of 10-byte entries. The first 2 bytes of each entry contain an EMM handle, and the next 8 bytes contain the name associated with the handle. Handles that have never been assigned a name have 8 bytes of 00H as a name.

■ Because the maximum number of active handles is 255, the buffer need not be longer than 2550 bytes.

EMS Function 54H (84) [4.0]
Subfunction 01H
Search for Handle Name

Returns the EMM handle associated with the specified name.

Call with:

AH	= 54H
AL	= 01H
DS:SI	= segment:offset of 8-byte handle name

Returns:

If function successful

AH	= 00H
DX	= EMM handle

If function unsuccessful

AH	= error code

EMS Function 54H (84) [4.0]
Subfunction 02H
Get Total Handles

Returns the total number of handles supported by the EMM, including the operating-system handle (0).

Call with:

AH	= 54H
AL	= 02H

Returns:

If function successful

AH	= 00H
BX	= number of handles

If function unsuccessful

AH	= error code

EMS Function 55H (85)   [4.0]
Subfunctions 00H and 01H
Map Pages and Jump

Alters the expanded memory mapping context, and transfers control to the specified address.

Call with:

AH	= 55H
AL	= subfunction
	00H = map using physical page numbers
	01H = map using physical page segments
DX	= EMM handle
DS:SI	= segment:offset of buffer (see Notes)

Returns:

If function successful
AH   = 00H

If function unsuccessful
AH   = error code

Notes:

■ The format of the buffer containing map and jump entries is:

Offset	Length	Description
00H	4	far pointer to jump target
04H	1	number of pages to map before jump
05H	4	far pointer to map list (see below)

The map list in turn consists of DWORD (32-bit) entries, one per page. The first word of each entry contains the logical page number, and the second word contains the physical page number or segment (depending on the value in register AL) to which it should be mapped.

■ A request to map 0 pages and jump is not an error; the effect is a simple far jump.

EMS Function 56H (86)   [4.0]
Subfunctions 00H and 01H
Map Pages and Call

Alters the expanded memory mapping context, and performs a far call to the specified address. When the destination routine executes a far return, the EMM again alters the page-mapping context as instructed and then returns control to the original caller.

Call with:

AH	= 56H
AL	= subfunction
	00H = map using physical page numbers
	01H = map using physical page segments
DX	= EMM handle
DS:SI	= segment:offset of buffer (see Notes)

Returns:

If function successful
AH   = 00H

If function unsuccessful
AH   = error code

Notes:

■ The format of the buffer containing map and call information is:

Offset	Length	Description
00H	4	far pointer to call target
04H	1	number of pages to map before call
05H	4	far pointer to list of pages to map before call (see below)
09H	1	number of pages to map before return
0AH	4	far pointer to list of pages to map before return (see below)
0EH	8	reserved (0)

Both map lists have the same format and consist of a series of double-word entries, one per page. The first word of each entry contains the logical page number, and the second word contains the physical page number or segment (depending on the value in register AL) to which it should be mapped.

■ A request to map 0 pages and call is not an error; the effect is a simple far call.

- This function uses extra stack space to save information about the mapping context; the amount of stack space required can be determined by calling EMS Function 56H Subfunction 02H.

EMS Function 56H (86) [4.0]
Subfunction 02H
Get Stack Space for Map Page and Call

Returns the number of bytes of stack space required by EMS Function 56H Subfunction 00H or 01H.

Call with:

AH	= 56H
AL	= 02H

Returns:

If function successful

AH	= 00H
BX	= stack space required (bytes)

If function unsuccessful

AH	= error code

EMS Function 57H (87) [4.0]
Subfunction 00H
Move Memory Region

Copies a memory region from any location in conventional or expanded memory to any other, without disturbing the current expanded memory mapping context.

Call with:

AH	= 57H
AL	= 00H
DS:SI	= segment:offset of buffer (see Notes)

Returns:

If function successful
AH   = 00H

If function unsuccessful
AH   = error code

Notes:

■ The format of the buffer controlling the move operation is:

Offset	Length	Description
00H	4	region length (in bytes)
04H	1	source memory type (0 = conventional, 1 = expanded)
05H	2	source memory handle
07H	2	source memory offset
09H	2	source memory segment or logical page number
0BH	1	destination memory type (0 = conventional, 1 = expanded)
0CH	2	destination memory handle
0EH	2	destination memory offset
10H	2	destination memory segment or logical page number

■ A length of 0 bytes is not an error. The maximum length of a move is 1 MB. If the length exceeds a single EMM page, consecutive EMM pages (as many as are required) supply or receive the data.

■ If the source and destination addresses overlap, the move will be performed in such a way that the destination receives an intact copy of the original data, and a nonzero status is returned.

EMS Function 57H (87)   [4.0]
Subfunction 01H
Exchange Memory Regions

Exchanges any two memory regions in conventional or expanded memory, without disturbing the current expanded memory mapping context.

Call with:

AH   = 57H
AL   = 01H
DS:SI   = segment:offset of buffer (see Notes)

Returns:

If function successful
AH   = 00H

If function unsuccessful
AH   = error code

Notes:

■ The format of the buffer controlling the exchange operation is the same as for EMS Function 57H Subfunction 00H.

■ An exchange of 0 bytes is not an error. The maximum length of an exchange is 1 MB. If the length exceeds a single EMM page, consecutive EMM pages (as many as are required) supply or receive the data.

■ If the source and destination addresses overlap, the exchange is not performed and an error is returned.

EMS Function 58H (88)   [4.0]
Subfunction 00H
Get Addresses of Mappable Pages

Returns the segment base address and physical page number for each mappable page in the system.

Call with:

AH   = 58H
AL   = 00H
ES:DI   = segment:offset of buffer (see Notes)

Returns:

If function successful
AH   = 00H
CX   = number of entries in mappable physical page array

and page number/address information in buffer (see Notes)

If function unsuccessful
AH   = error code

Notes:

■ Upon return from the function, the buffer contains a series of double-word entries, one per mappable page. The first word of an entry contains the page's segment base address, and the second word contains its physical page number. The entries are sorted in order of ascending segment addresses.

■ The size of the buffer required can be calculated with the information returned by EMS Function 58H Subfunction 01H.

EMS Function 58H (88)   [4.0]
Subfunction 01H
Get Number of Mappable Pages

Returns the number of mappable physical pages.

Call with:

AH	= 58H
AL	= 01H

Returns:

If function successful

AH	= 00H
CX	= number of mappable physical pages

If function unsuccessful

AH	= error code

Note:

■ The information returned by this function can be used to calculate the size of the buffer that will be needed by EMS Function 58H Subfunction 00H.

EMS Function 59H (89)   [4.0]
Subfunction 00H
Get Hardware Configuration

Returns information about the configuration of the expanded memory hardware.

Call with:

AH	= 59H
AL	= 00H
ES:DI	= segment:offset of buffer (see Notes)

Returns:

If function successful
AH   = 00H

and hardware configuration information in buffer.

If function unsuccessful
AH   = error code

Notes:

■ Upon return from the function, the format of the buffer containing hardware configuration information is:

Offset	Length	Description
00H	2	size of raw EMM pages (in paragraphs)
02H	2	number of alternate register sets
04H	2	size of mapping-context save area (in bytes)
06H	2	number of register sets that can be assigned to DMA channels
08H	2	DMA operation type (0 = DMA can be used with alternate register sets; 1 = only one DMA register set available)

■ The size returned for the mapping-context save area is the same as the size returned by EMS Function 4EH Subfunction 03H.

■ This function is intended for an operating system only and can be disabled by the operating system at any time.

EMS Function 59H (89)   [4.0]
Subfunction 01H
Get Number of Raw Pages

Obtains the total number of raw EMM pages present in the system and the number of raw pages that are not already allocated. Raw EMM pages can have a size other than 16 KB.

Call with:

AH   = 59H
AL   = 01H

Returns:

If function successful
AH   = 00H
BX   = unallocated raw pages
DX   = total raw pages

If function unsuccessful
AH   = error code

Note:

- If the EMM supports only pages of standard size, the values returned by this function are the same as those returned by EMS Function 42H.

EMS Function 5AH (90)   [4.0]
Subfunction 00H
Allocate Handle and Standard Pages

Allocates an EMM handle and associates standard (16 KB) EMM pages with that handle.

Call with:

AH   = 5AH
AL   = 00H
BX   = number of standard pages to allocate

Returns:

If function successful
AH   = 00H
DX   = EMM handle

If function unsuccessful
AH   = error code

Note:

- Allocating 0 pages with this function is not an error, as it is with EMS Function 43H.

EMS Function 5AH (90)   [4.0]
Subfunction 01H
Allocate Handle and Raw Pages

Allocates a raw EMM handle and associates raw EMM pages with that handle.

Call with:

AH	= 5AH
AL	= 01H
BX	= number of raw pages to allocate

Returns:

If function successful

AH	= 00H
DX	= handle for raw EMM pages

If function unsuccessful

AH	= error code

Notes:

■ Raw EMM pages can have a size other than 16 KB.

■ Allocating 0 pages with this function is not an error.

EMS Function 5BH (90)   [4.0]
Subfunction 00H
Get Alternate Map Registers

Returns the number of the active alternate register set, or (if an alternate set is not active) saves the state of the mapping registers into a buffer and returns its address.

Call with:

AH	= 5BH
AL	= 00H

Returns:

If function successful and alternate map register set active

AH	= 00H
BL	= current active alternate map register set number

If function successful and alternate map register set not active

AH   = 00H
BL   = 00H
ES:DI   = segment:offset of alternate map register save area

If function unsuccessful

AH   = error code

Notes:

■ The address of the save area must have been specified in a previous call to EMS Function 5BH Subfunction 01H, and the save area must have been initialized by a previous call to EMS Function 4EH Subfunction 00H. If no previous call was made to EMS Function 5BH Subfunction 01H, the address returned is 0 and the registers are not saved.

■ This function is intended for an operating system only and can be disabled by the operating system at any time.

EMS Function 5BH (91)   [4.0]
Subfunction 01H
Set Alternate Map Registers

Selects an alternate map register set, or (if alternate sets are not supported) restores the mapping context from the specified buffer.

Call with:

AH   = 5BH
AL   = 01H
BL   = alternate register set number or 00H
ES:DI   = segment:offset of map register context buffer
            (if BL = 0)

Returns:

If function successful

AH   = 00H

If function unsuccessful

AH   = error code

Notes:

■ The buffer address specified in this call is returned by subsequent calls to EMS Function 5BH Subfunction 00H with BL = 00H.

- The buffer must have been initialized by a previous call to EMS Function 4EH Subfunction 00H.

- This function is intended for an operating system only and can be disabled by the operating system at any time.

EMS Function 5BH (91)   [4.0]
Subfunction 02H
Get Size of Alternate Map Register Save Area

Returns the amount of storage needed by EMS Function 5BH Subfunctions 00H and 01H.

Call with:

```
AH      = 5BH
AL      = 02H
```

Returns:

If function successful
```
AH      = 00H
DX      = size of buffer (bytes)
```

If function unsuccessful
```
AH      = error code
```

Note:

- This function is intended for an operating system only and can be disabled by the operating system at any time.

EMS Function 5BH (91)   [4.0]
Subfunction 03H
Allocate Alternate Map Register Set

Allocates an alternate map register set for use with EMS Function 5BH Subfunctions 00H and 01H. The contents of the currently active map registers are copied into the newly allocated alternate map registers in order to provide an initial context when they are selected.

Call with:

AH   = 5BH
AL   = 03H

Returns:

If function successful
AH   = 00H
BL   = alternate map register set number, or 0 (if alternate
         sets are not available)

If function unsuccessful
AH   = error code

Note:

■ This function is intended for an operating system only and can be disabled by the operating system at any time.

EMS Function 5BH (91)   [4.0]
Subfunction 04H
Deallocate Alternate Map Register Set

Releases an alternate map register set that was previously allocated with EMS Function 5BH Subfunction 03H.

Call with:

AH   = 5BH
AL   = 04H
BL   = alternate register set number

Returns:

If function successful
AH   = 00H
If function unsuccessful
AH   = error code

Notes:

■ The current alternate map register set cannot be deallocated.

■ This function is intended for an operating system only and can be disabled by the operating system at any time.

EMS Function 5BH (91) [4.0]
Subfunction 05H
Allocate DMA Register Set

Allocates a DMA register set.

Call with:

AH	= 5BH
AL	= 05H

Returns:

If function successful

AH	= 00H
BL	= DMA register set number (0 = none available)

If function unsuccessful

AH	= error code

Note:

■ This function is intended for an operating system only and can be disabled by the operating system at any time.

EMS Function 5BH (91) [4.0]
Subfunction 06H
Enable DMA on Alternate Map Register Set

Associates a DMA channel with an alternate map register set.

Call with:

AH	= 5BH
AL	= 06H
BL	= alternate map register set
DL	= DMA channel number

Returns:

If function successful

AH	= 00H

If function unsuccessful

AH	= error code

Notes:

■ If a DMA channel is not assigned to a specific register set, DMA for that channel will be mapped through the current register set.

■ If 0 is specified as the alternate map register set, no special action is taken on DMA accesses for the specified DMA channel.

■ This function is intended for an operating system only and can be disabled by the operating system at any time.

EMS Function 5BH (91)   [4.0]
Subfunction 07H
Disable DMA on Alternate Map Register Set

Disables DMA accesses for all DMA channels that were associated with a specific alternate map register set.

Call with:

AH	= 5BH
AL	= 07H
BL	= alternate register set number

Returns:

If function successful
AH   = 00H

If function unsuccessful
AH   = error code

Note:

■ This function is intended for an operating system only and can be disabled by the operating system at any time.

EMS Function 5BH (91)   [4.0]
Subfunction 08H
Deallocate DMA Register Set

Deallocates a DMA register set that was previously allocated with EMS Function 5BH Subfunction 05H.

Call with:

AH   = 5BH
AL   = 08H
BL   = DMA register set number

Returns:

If function successful
AH   = 00H

If function unsuccessful
AH   = error code

Note:

■ This function is intended for an operating system only and can be disabled by the operating system at any time.

EMS Function 5CH (92)   [4.0]
Prepare EMM for Warm Boot

Prepares the expanded memory hardware for an impending warm boot. This function affects the current mapping context, the alternate register set in use, and any other expanded memory hardware dependencies that would ordinarily be initialized at system boot time.

Call with:

AH   = 5CH

Returns:

If function successful
AH   = 00H

If function unsuccessful
AH   = error code

Note:

■ If an application maps expanded memory at addresses below 640 KB, the application must trap all possible conditions that might lead to a warm boot so that this function can be called first.

EMS Function 5DH (93)   [4.0]
Subfunction 00H
Enable EMM Operating-System Functions

Enables the operating-system–specific EMM functions (EMS Functions 59H, 5BH, and 5DH) for calls by any program or device driver. (This is the default condition.)

Call with:

AH   = 5DH
AL   = 00H
BX:CX = access key (if not first call to function)

Returns:

If function successful
AH   = 00H
BX:CX = access key (if first call to function)

If function unsuccessful
AH   = error code

Notes:

- An access key is returned in registers BX and CX on the first call to EMS Function 5DH Subfunction 00H or 01H. The access key is required for all subsequent calls to either function.

- This function is intended for an operating system only.

EMS Function 5DH (93)   [4.0]
Subfunction 01H
Disable EMM Operating-System Functions

Disables the operating-system–specific EMM functions (EMS Functions 59H, 5BH, and 5DH) for calls by application programs and device drivers, reserving the use of these functions for the operating system.

Call with:

AH   = 5DH
AL   = 01H
BX:CX = access key (if not first call to function)

Returns:

If function successful
AH   = 00H
BX:CX   = access key (if first call to function)

If function unsuccessful
AH   = error code

Notes:

■ An access key is returned in registers BX and CX on the first call to EMS Function 5DH Subfunction 00H or 01H. The access key is required for all subsequent calls to either function.

■ This function is intended for an operating system only.

EMS Function 5DH (93)   [4.0]
Subfunction 02H
Release Access Key

Releases the access key obtained by a previous call to EMS Function 5DH Subfunction 00H or 01H.

Call with:

AH   = 5DH
AL   = 02H
BX:CX   = access key

Returns:

If function successful
AH   = 00H

If function unsuccessful
AH   = error code

Notes:

■ With respect to the operating-system–specific expanded memory functions, the EMM is returned to the state that it had when the system was initialized. A new access key will be returned by the next call to EMS Function 5DH Subfunction 00H or 01H.

■ This function is intended for an operating system only and can be disabled by the operating system at any time.

eXtended Memory Specification (XMS)

The eXtended Memory Specification (XMS) defines a software interface that allows real-mode application programs to use extended memory, as well as certain areas of conventional memory that are not ordinarily managed by MS-DOS, in a cooperative and hardware-independent manner. The XMS allows applications to allocate, resize, and release memory blocks of three basic types:

- The "high memory area" (HMA) at addresses between 1024 KB and 1088 KB
- Extended memory blocks (EMBs) from addresses above 1088 KB
- Upper memory blocks (UMBs) at addresses between 640 KB and 1024 KB (1 MB)

The XMS also provides hardware-independent control over the A20 address line, which must be enabled to read or write the HMA in real mode. An installable device driver that implements the XMS is called an eXtended Memory Manager (XMM).

Driver Installation

The prototype XMM provided by Microsoft, named HIMEM.SYS, is installed by adding a DEVICE= line to the CONFIG.SYS file and rebooting the system. HIMEM.SYS accepts two optional switches:

/HMAMIN=n	specifies the minimum number of KB in the HMA that a program can use (0–63, default = 0)
/NUMHANDLES=n	sets the maximum number of XMS handles that can be active at any one time (0–128, default = 32)

Some 80386-specific memory managers—Qualitas's 386MAX.SYS, for example—can provide both EMS-compatible and XMS-compatible services in the same driver. In such cases, additional loading of HIMEM.SYS is not required. All XMMs require MS-DOS version 3.0 or later.

Determining Presence of Driver

A program can determine whether an XMS-compatible driver is available by setting AX to 4300H and executing an Int 2FH. If the driver is present, the value 80H is returned in AL; if the driver is absent, AL will be returned unchanged or with some other value.

```
                            ; check if driver available
        mov     ax,4300h    ; 4300H = get install state
        int     2fh         ; call driver
        cmp     al,80h      ; status = installed?
        je      present     ; yes, driver is present
        jmp     absent      ; no, driver is absent
```

Note that this convention differs from that used by the MS-DOS extensions PRINT, SHARE, ASSIGN, and APPEND, which are also accessed via Int 2FH (using other values in AH). These four extensions return AL = FFH if they are already installed.

Using Driver Functions

After a program has established that the XMS driver is available, it obtains the entry point of the driver by executing Int 2FH with AX = 4310H. The entry point is returned in registers ES:BX and must be saved in a variable.

```
xmsaddr dd      ?                   ; receives entry point
        .
        .
        .
                            ; get address of XMS
                            ; driver entry point...
        mov     ax,4310h    ; function 43H subfunction 10H
        int     2fh         ; call driver
                            ; save far pointer
                            ; to entry point...
        mov     word ptr xmsaddr,bx
        mov     word ptr xmsaddr+2,es
```

With the entry point in hand, the program enters the driver by a far call, without further resort to Int 2FH. A particular XMS function is selected by the value in AH. Other parameters are passed in registers.

```
xmsaddr dd      ?                   ; receives entry point
        .
        .
        .
                            ; request XMS function...
        mov     ah,function ; AH = function number
        .                   ; load other registers with
        .                   ; function-specific values
        call    [xmsaddr]   ; indirect far call to driver
```

At least 256 bytes of stack space should be available when requesting an XMS function.

Most XMS functions return a status in register AX: 0001H if the function succeeded or 0000H if the function failed. In the latter case, an error code is also returned in register BL with the high bit set. Other results typically are also passed back in registers.

Warning: Some XMMs support only a subset of XMS functions.

HMA Usage Guidelines

The HMA is extended memory that can be addressed directly by a program running in real mode. The program must enable the A20 line (see XMS Function 03H) and then address the memory using a segment register that contains the value FFFFH. In other words, the HMA lies at addresses FFFF:0010H through FFFFH:FFFFH.

The HMA is always allocated as a unit. A device driver or TSR program that uses the HMA should store as much of its code there as possible, because the remainder of the HMA will simply be lost for use by other programs. If the driver or TSR cannot exploit nearly all of the HMA, it should leave HMA available for use by subsequently loaded programs. The user can enforce such ''good behavior'' with the /HMAMIN switch.

Device drivers and TSRs must not leave the A20 line permanently turned on. Some applications rely on the wrapping of memory addresses at the 1 MB boundary and will overwrite the HMA if the A20 line is left enabled. Similarly, interrupt vectors must not point directly into the HMA, because the A20 line will not necessarily be enabled at the time that the interrupt is received.

If the HMA is still available when a normal application runs, the application is free to use as much or as little of the HMA as it wants, with the following restrictions:

- Far pointers to data located in the HMA cannot be passed to MS-DOS.

- Disk I/O directly into the HMA by any method is not recommended.

The application can ensure that it receives control of the HMA if the HMA is not already in use by calling the allocation function with a special value (see XMS Function 01H). The application must be sure to release the HMA before it terminates; otherwise, the HMA will be unavailable for use by any other programs until the system is restarted.

Reference

The XMS is a collaborative effort of Microsoft Corporation, Intel Corporation, Lotus Development Corporation, and AST Research Inc. The information in this section has been checked against the eXtended

Memory Specification version 2.0, dated July 19, 1988. This document
is available from Microsoft Corporation, Box 97017, Redmond,
Washington, 98073.

XMS Error Codes

If an XMS function returns AX = 0000H, and bit 7 of BL = 1, an error
has occurred. In that case, the contents of BL are interpreted as
follows:

Error code	Meaning
80H	Function was not implemented
81H	VDISK device driver was detected
82H	A20 error occurred
8EH	General driver error occurred
8FH	Unrecoverable driver error occurred
90H	HMA does not exist
91H	HMA is already in use
92H	DX is less than /HMAMIN= parameter
93H	HMA is not allocated
94H	A20 line is still enabled
A0H	All extended memory is allocated
A1H	EMM handles are exhausted
A2H	Handle is invalid
A3H	Source handle is invalid
A4H	Source offset is invalid
A5H	Destination handle is invalid
A6H	Destination offset is invalid
A7H	Length is invalid
A8H	Overlap in move request is invalid
A9H	Parity error was detected
AAH	Block is not locked
ABH	Block is locked
ACH	Lock count overflowed
ADH	Lock failed
B0H	Smaller UMB is available
B1H	No UMBs are available
B2H	UMB segment number is invalid

Summary of XMS Functions

Function   *Name*

Driver information

00H   Get XMS Version

HMA management

01H   Allocate HMA
02H   Free HMA

A20 line management

03H   Global Enable A20 Line
04H   Global Disable A20 Line
05H   Local Enable A20 Line
06H   Local Disable A20 Line
07H   Query A20 Line State

EMB management

08H   Query Free Extended Memory
09H   Allocate EMB
0AH   Free EMB
0BH   Move EMB
0CH   Lock EMB
0DH   Unlock EMB
0EH   Get Handle Information
0FH   Resize EMB

UMB management

10H   Allocate UMB
11H   Free UMB

XMS Function 00H
Get XMS Version

Returns the XMM version number, the version of XMS it supports, and a code indicating whether the HMA exists.

Call with:

AH   = 00H

Returns:

If function successful

AX   = XMS version supported
BX   = driver version
DX   = HMA indicator
            0000H if no HMA
            0001H if HMA exists

If function unsuccessful

AX   = 0000H
BL   = error code

Notes:

■ The version numbers returned in AX and BX are binary-coded decimal (BCD). For example, if the function returns AX = 0235H, the driver is compatible with the XMS version 2.35.

■ The value returned in DX is not affected by any previous allocation of the HMA by another program.

XMS Function 01H
Allocate High Memory Area

Reserves the entire HMA for use by the calling program.

Call with:

AH   = 01H
DX   = HMA bytes needed (if caller is device driver or TSR)
            FFFFH (if caller is application program)

Returns:

If function successful (HMA was assigned to caller)

AX   = 0001H

If function unsuccessful

AX   = 0000H
BL   = error code

Notes:

■ The HMA is a maximum of 64 KB − 16 (65,520) bytes in size, and its base address is FFFF:0010H.

■ The function fails if the HMA has already been reserved by another program or if the requested size is smaller than the XMS driver's /HMAMIN parameter.

- If an application program fails to release the HMA before it terminates, the HMA becomes unavailable for use by any other programs until the system is restarted.

XMS Function 02H
Free High Memory Area

Releases the HMA that was previously reserved with XMS Function 01H.

Call with:

AH   = 02H

Returns:

If function successful
AX   = 0001H

If function unsuccessful
AX   = 0000H
BL   = error code

XMS Function 03H
Global Enable A20 Line

Enables the A20 address line. This function should only be used by programs that have successfully allocated the HMA with XMS Function 01H.

Call with:

AH   = 03H

Returns:

If function successful (A20 line was enabled)
AX   = 0001H

If function unsuccessful
AX   = 0000H
BL   = error code

Notes:

- The calling program should disable the A20 line with XMS Function 04H before releasing control of the system.

■ See also XMS Functions 05H and 06H, which can be used by programs that do not control the HMA.

XMS Function 04H
Global Disable A20 Line

Disables the A20 address line, canceling the effect of a previous call to XMS Function 03H. This function should only be used by programs that have successfully allocated the HMA with XMS Function 01H.

Call with:

AH = 04H

Returns:

If function successful (A20 line was disabled)
AX = 0001H

If function unsuccessful
AX = 0000H
BL = error code

Note:

■ See also XMS Functions 05H and 06H, which can be used by programs that do not control the HMA.

XMS Function 05H
Local Enable A20 Line

Enables the A20 address line, allowing direct access to extended memory.

Call with:

AH = 05H

Returns:

If function successful (A20 line was enabled)
AX = 0001H

If function unsuccessful
AX = 0000H
BL = error code

Notes:

■ The calling program should disable the A20 line with XMS Function 06H before releasing control of the system.

■ See also XMS Functions 03H and 04H, which can be used by programs that control the HMA.

XMS Function 06H
Local Disable A20 Line

Disables the A20 address line, canceling the effect of a previous call to XMS Function 05H.

Call with:

AH   = 06H

Returns:

If function successful (A20 line was disabled)
AX   = 0001H

If function unsuccessful
AX   = 0000H
BL   = error code

Note:

■ See also XMS Functions 03H and 04H, which can be used by programs that control the HMA.

XMS Function 07H
Query A20 Line State

Returns the current state of the A20 address line.

Call with:

AH   = 07H

Returns:

If A20 line is enabled
AX   = 0001H

If A20 line is disabled
AX   = 0000H
BL   = 00H

If function unsuccessful
AX   = 0000H
BL   = error code

XMS Function 08H
Query Free Extended Memory

Returns the size of the largest free EMB and the total amount of free extended memory.

Call with:

AH   = 08H

Returns:

If function successful
AX   = size of largest free block (KB)
DX   = total free extended memory (KB)

If function unsuccessful
AX   = 0000H
BL   = error code

Note:

■ The HMA is not included in the returned values, even if it is not in use.

XMS Function 09H
Allocate Extended Memory Block

Allocates an EMB, and returns a handle that can be used for subsequent access to the memory.

Call with:

AH   = 09H
DX   = requested block size (KB)

Returns:

If function successful (memory was allocated)
AX   = 0001H
DX   = EMB handle

If function unsuccessful
AX   = 0000H
BL   = error code

Notes:

■ An EMB block length of 0 is explicitly allowed.

■ EMB handles are scarce resources; a program should attempt to minimize the number of handles in use at any one time.

XMS Function 0AH (10)
Free Extended Memory Block

Releases an EMB that was previously allocated with XMS Function 09H.

Call with:

AH   = 0AH
DX   = EMB handle

Returns:

If function successful
AX   = 0001H

If function unsuccessful
AX   = 0000H
BL   = error code

Note:

■ If a program fails to release its EMBs before it terminates, those blocks and their associated handles become unavailable for use by other programs until the system is restarted.

XMS Function 0BH (11)
Move Extended Memory Block

Copies a region from any location in conventional or extended memory to any other location.

Call with:

AH	= 0BH
DS:SI	= segment:offset of parameter block (see Notes)

Returns:

If function successful

AX	= 0001H

If function unsuccessful

AX	= 0000H
BL	= error code

Notes:

- The structure of the parameter block is as follows:

Offset	Length	Description
00H	4	Length of EMB (in bytes; must be even)
04H	2	Source EMB handle
06H	4	32-bit offset within source block
0AH	2	Destination EMB handle
0CH	4	32-bit offset within destination block

The source and destination handles must have been obtained by a previous call to XMS Function 09H. Neither handle need be locked before calling this function.

- If the source and/or destination handle is 0, the corresponding 32-bit offset field is interpreted as a segment:offset (far pointer) in the standard Intel format.

- The speed of the move operation can be maximized by using word-aligned source and destination offsets on 80286 machines and double-word–aligned offsets on 80386 machines.

- If the source and destination regions overlap, the move is not guaranteed to work correctly unless the source address is less than the destination address.

- Programs should not enable the A20 line before calling this function. The state of the A20 line is preserved.

- The function provides interrupt windows at suitable intervals during long transfers.

XMS Function 0CH (12)
Lock Extended Memory Block

Locks an EMB, and returns the 32-bit linear base address of the block.
Lock calls can be nested.

Call with:

AH   = 0CH
DX   = EMB handle

Returns:

If function successful
AX   = 0001H
DX:BX   = 32-bit linear address of locked block

If function unsuccessful
AX   = 0000H
BL   = error code

Note:

■ This function is intended for use by programs that enable the A20
line and then address EMBs directly. EMBs need not be locked
before calls to XMS Function 0BH.

XMS Function 0DH (13)
Unlock Extended Memory Block

Unlocks an EMB that was previously locked with XMS Function
0CH.

Call with:

AH   = 0DH
DX   = EMB handle

Returns:

If function successful
AX   = 0001H

If function unsuccessful
AX   = 0000H
BL   = error code

Note:

- After this function is called, the 32-bit linear address previously returned by Function 0CH for the EMB becomes invalid and should not be used. The XMM can move the EMB while it is unlocked to satisfy other allocation requests.

XMS Function 0EH (14)
Get Handle Information

Returns information about an EMB handle.

Call with:

AH   = 0EH
DX   = EMB handle

Returns:

If function successful
AX   = 0001H
BH   = lock count (0 if block is not locked)
BL   = number of handles still available
DX   = block size (KB)

If function unsuccessful
AX   = 0000H
BL   = error code

Note:

- The current base address of an EMB can be obtained by locking it with XMS Function 0CH.

XMS Function 0FH (15)
Resize Extended Memory Block

Changes the size of a previously allocated EMB. The function fails if the block is locked, because the XMM must be free to move the block (if necessary) in order to resize it.

Call with:

AH	= 0FH
BX	= new block size (KB)
DX	= EMB handle

Returns:

If function successful

AX	= 0001H

If function unsuccessful

AX	= 0000H
BL	= error code

XMS Function 10H (16)
Allocate Upper Memory Block

Allocates a UMB. A UMB is below the 1 MB boundary but above the conventional memory area controlled by MS-DOS.

Call with:

AH	= 10H
DX	= requested block size (in paragraphs)

Returns:

If function successful

AX	= 0001H
BX	= segment base of allocated block
DX	= actual block size (in paragraphs)

If function unsuccessful

AX	= 0000H
BL	= error code
DX	= size of largest available block (in paragraphs)

Notes:

■ UMBs are always paragraph-aligned.

■ The A20 line need not be enabled to access a UMB.

XMS Function 11H (17)
Free Upper Memory Block

Releases a UMB that was previously allocated with XMS Function 10H.

Call with:

AH   = 11H
DX   = segment base of block

Returns:

If function successful
AX   = 0001H

If function unsuccessful
AX   = 0000H
BL   = error code

Microsoft CD-ROM Extensions

The Microsoft CD-ROM Extensions allow MS-DOS applications to access CD-ROMs in the High Sierra or ISO-9660 formats as if they were standard MS-DOS block devices. An entire CD-ROM is represented as a single logical unit with up to 660 MB of storage, and files can be opened and read with normal Int 21H function calls. The CD-ROM Extensions also support a set of special function calls, described in this section, that provide applications with CD-ROM–specific information.

An icon in each function heading indicates the version of Microsoft CD-ROM Extensions in which that function was first supported. You can assume that the function is available in all subsequent versions unless explicitly noted otherwise.

Driver Installation

Support for CD-ROMs in an MS-DOS system requires two separate software components. The first is a hardware-specific device driver for the CD-ROM drive, usually supplied by the drive's manufacturer. The device driver is installed with a DEVICE= directive in the CONFIG.SYS file. The logical name for the drive is specified with a /D switch in the DEVICE= line; other switches are OEM-dependent.

The Microsoft MS-DOS CD-ROM Extensions are supplied in the file MSCDEX.EXE and are loaded as a terminate-and-stay-resident utility, usually by adding a line to the AUTOEXEC.BAT file on the boot drive. MSCDEX requires MS-DOS version 3.1 or later because it makes use of the "redirector" hooks that were added in version 3.1 to support MS Networks. If any network software is being used, it must be loaded before MSCDEX.

MSCDEX accepts a number of different switches on its command line:

/D:*name* Notifies MSCDEX of the logical name previously assigned to the CD-ROM installable device driver(s). More than one /D switch can be present (one for each logical unit).

(continued)

/E	Requests that MSCDEX use expanded memory if it is available.
/K	Configures MSCDEX to handle Kanji volumes.
/L:*x*	Notifies MSCDEX to start assigning CD-ROM logical units with drive letter *x*.
/M:*n*	Specifies the number of buffers that MSCDEX will allocate to cache CD-ROM sectors. Larger numbers will result in less directory thrashing and better performance.
/S	Causes MSCDEX to patch MS-DOS, allowing CD-ROMs to be shared on network servers.
/V	Requests "verbose" mode; information about memory usage is displayed during MSCDEX installation.

One or more /D switches must always be present. Some of the switches listed above might not be supported in MSCDEX versions prior to 2.10.

Determining Presence of Driver

An application program can determine whether the MS CD-ROM Extensions are available and whether one or more CD-ROM drives are present by setting AX to 1500H and BX to 0000H and executing an Int 2FH. If BX is nonzero on return, MSCDEX is installed and at least one CD-ROM drive exists; if BX is 0, MSCDEX is absent or no CD-ROM units exist.

```
mov     ax,1500h        ; check if CD-ROM available
xor     bx,bx
int     2fh             ; invoke MSCDEX
or      bx,bx           ; one or more CD-ROMs?
jnz     present         ; yes, CD-ROMs are present
jmp     absent          ; no CD-ROMs or MSCDEX
```

Note that this convention differs from that used by the MS-DOS extensions PRINT, SHARE, ASSIGN, and APPEND to check installed state.

Using Driver Functions

After the presence of MSCDEX has been verified, its functions are invoked by executing an Int 2FH with 15H in register AH and a function number in AL. Other parameters are usually passed in registers; for example, many functions require that register CX contain the drive code for the CD-ROM unit.

```
mov     ah,15h          ; AH = 15H for MSCDEX
mov     al,function     ; AL selects MSCDEX function
.                       ; load other registers with
.                       ; function-specific values
int     2fh             ; transfer to MSCDEX
```

MSCDEX returns the carry flag cleared if the function is successful.
Other results are typically passed back in registers, although a few
functions place data in a buffer specified by the calling program. The
carry flag is returned set if the function failed; in this case, AX contains a normal MS-DOS error code.

Reference

The information in this reference has been checked against the
Microsoft MS-DOS CD-ROM Extensions documentation, version 2.10,
dated December 20, 1988. You can obtain the High Sierra May 28th
Proposal ("Standard for Volume and File Structure of CD-ROM")
from the National Standards Organization, P.O. Box 1056, Bethesda,
MD 20817. You can obtain ISO-9660 ("Information Processing —
Volume and File Structure of CD-ROM for Information Interchange")
from the American National Standards Institute, 1430 Broadway, New
York, NY 10018. (Sales: 212-642-4900. Fax orders: 212-302-1286.)

Summary of CD-ROM Extensions Functions

Function(s)	Name
00H	Get Number of CD-ROM Drives
01H	Get CD-ROM Drive List
02H	Get Copyright Filename
03H	Get Abstract Filename
04H	Get Bibliographic Filename
05H	Read Volume Table of Contents
06H	Reserved
07H	Reserved
08H	Absolute Disk Read
09H	Absolute Disk Write

(continued)

Function(s)	Name
0AH	Reserved
0BH	CD-ROM Drive Check
0CH	Get CD-ROM Extensions Version
0DH	Get CD-ROM Units
0EH	Get or Set Volume Descriptor Preference
0FH	Get Directory Entry
10H	Send Device Request
11H–0FFH	Reserved

MSCDEX Function 00H   [1.0]
Get Number of CD-ROM Drives

Returns the total number of CD-ROM drives in the system.

Call with:

AH	= 15H
AL	= 00H
BX	= 0000H

Returns:

If CD-ROM extensions not installed

BX	= 0000H

If CD-ROM extensions installed

BX	= number of CD-ROM logical units
CX	= first CD-ROM logical drive (0 = A, 1 = B, etc.)

Note:

■ In a system that contains multiple CD-ROM drives and that is also networked, the CD-ROM drives might not be assigned as consecutive logical units. See also MSCDEX Function 0DH (Get CD-ROM Drive Letters).

MSCDEX Function 01H [1.0]
Get CD-ROM Drive List

Returns a driver unit identifier for each CD-ROM drive in the system, along with the address of the header for the device driver that controls the drive.

Call with:

AH	= 15H
AL	= 01H
ES:BX	= segment:offset of buffer

Returns:

Nothing (information placed in caller's buffer)

Notes:

■ The buffer is filled in with 5-byte entries in the following format:

Offset	Length	Description
00H	1	driver unit code
01H	2	offset of device driver header
03H	2	segment of device driver header

The driver unit code returned in the buffer is not the systemwide logical drive identifier but is the relative unit for that particular driver. For example, if three CD-ROM drivers are installed, each supporting one physical drive, the driver unit code in each 5-byte entry will be 0. The systemwide drive identifiers for each CD-ROM unit can be obtained with MSCDEX Function 0DH (Get CD-ROM Drive Letters).

■ The maximum buffer size that will ever be needed is 26 units × 5 bytes/unit, or 130 bytes. The actual size needed can be calculated from the information returned (in BX) by MSCDEX Function 00H.

MSCDEX Function 02H [1.0]
Get Copyright Filename

Returns the name of the copyright file from the volume table of contents (VTOC) of the specified CD-ROM drive.

Call with:

AH	= 15H
AL	= 02H
CX	= drive (0 = A, 1 = B, etc.)
ES:BX	= segment:offset of 38-byte buffer

Returns:

If function successful
Carry flag = clear

and filename placed in buffer as ASCIIZ string

If function unsuccessful (drive is not CD-ROM)
Carry flag = set
AX   = error code

Notes:

- The 38-byte buffer allows for a 31-character filename followed by a semicolon (;), a 5-digit version number, and a terminating NULL byte.

- On disks that comply with the High Sierra standard, the filename has an MS-DOS–compatible ⁸/₃ format.

MSCDEX Function 03H   [1.0]
Get Abstract Filename

Returns the name of the abstract file from the volume table of contents (VTOC) for the specified CD-ROM drive.

Call with:

AH	= 15H
AL	= 03H
CX	= drive (0 = A, 1 = B, etc.)
ES:BX	= segment:offset of 38-byte buffer

Returns:

If function successful
Carry flag = clear

and filename placed in buffer as ASCIIZ string

If function unsuccessful (drive is not CD-ROM)
Carry flag = set
AX   = error code

- The 38-byte buffer allows for a 31-character filename followed by a semicolon (;), a 5-digit version number, and a terminating NULL byte.

- On disks that comply with the High Sierra standard, the filename has an MS-DOS–compatible $^8/_3$ format.

MSCDEX Function 04H   [1.0]
Get Bibliographic Filename

Returns the name of the bibliographic file from the volume table of contents (VTOC) for the specified CD-ROM drive.

Call with:

AH	= 15H
AL	= 04H
CX	= drive (0 = A, 1 = B, etc.)
ES:BX	= segment:offset of 38-byte buffer

Returns:

If function successful
Carry flag = clear

and filename placed in buffer as ASCIIZ string

If function unsuccessful (drive is not CD-ROM)
Carry flag = set
AX   = error code

Notes:

- The 38-byte buffer allows for a 31-character filename followed by a semicolon (;), a 5-digit version number, and a terminating NULL byte.

- This function is provided for compatibility with the ISO-9660 standard. A null string is returned for disks complying with the High Sierra standard.

MSCDEX Function 05H [1.0]
Read Volume Table of Contents

Scans the descriptors that constitute the volume table of contents (VTOC) of a CD-ROM.

Call with:

AH	= 15H
AL	= 05H
CX	= drive (0 = A, 1 = B, etc.)
DX	= descriptor index (0, 1, etc.)
ES:BX	= segment:offset of 2048-byte buffer

Returns:

If function successful
Carry flag = clear
AX = descriptor type

00H = *descriptor other than standard or terminator*
01H = *standard volume descriptor*
FFH = *volume descriptor terminator*

and descriptor placed in calling program's buffer

If function unsuccessful
Carry flag = set
AX = error code

MSCDEX Function 06H
Reserved

This function is used for debugging purposes in some versions of MSCDEX, but it should not be called by normal application programs.

MSCDEX Function 07H
Reserved

This function is used for debugging purposes in some versions of MSCDEX, but it should not be called by normal application programs.

MSCDEX Function 08H [1.0]
Absolute Disk Read

Reads one or more logical sectors from a CD-ROM, bypassing the file system.

Call with:

AH	= 15H
AL	= 08H
CX	= drive (0 = A, 1 = B, etc.)
DX	= number of sectors to read
SI:DI	= starting sector
ES:BX	= segment:offset of buffer

Returns:

If function successful
Carry flag = clear

If function unsuccessful
Carry flag = set
AX   = error code

Note:

■ This function is analogous to the MS-DOS Int 25H function for direct access to logical sectors of floppy disks and fixed disks. Unlike Int 25H, however, this function does not require that an additional word be cleared from the stack after it returns.

MSCDEX Function 09H [1.0]
Absolute Disk Write

Writes one or more logical sectors, bypassing the file system. This function is not supported on CD-ROM media, but it is defined for use in authoring systems that build a CD-ROM file structure on a writable medium.

Call with:

AH	= 15H
AL	= 09H
CX	= drive (0 = A, 1 = B, etc.)
DX	= number of sectors to write

(continued)

SI:DI   = starting sector
ES:BX   = segment:offset of buffer

Returns:

If function successful
Carry flag = clear

If function unsuccessful
Carry flag = set
AX   = error code

Note:

- This function is analogous to the MS-DOS Int 26H function for direct access to logical sectors of floppy disks and fixed disks. Unlike Int 26H, however, this function does not require that an additional word be cleared from the stack after it returns.

MSCDEX Function 0AH
Reserved

MSCDEX Function 0BH   [2.0]
CD-ROM Drive Check

Returns a code indicating whether a particular logical unit is supported by the Microsoft CD-ROM Extensions module (MSCDEX).

Call with:

AH   = 15H
AL   = 0BH
BX   = 0000H
CX   = drive (0 = A, 1 = B, etc.)

Returns:

If MSCDEX installed, drive is CD-ROM
AX   < > 0000H
BX   = ADADH

If MSCDEX installed, drive is not CD-ROM

AX   = 0000H

BX   = ADADH

If MSCDEX not installed

BX   < > ADADH

MSCDEX Function 0CH   [2.0]
Get CD-ROM Extensions Version

Returns the version number of the Microsoft CD-ROM Extensions
module (MSCDEX).

Call with:

AH   = 15H

AL   = 0CH

BX   = 0000H

Returns:

If version 1.0x

BX   = 0000H

If version 2.00 or later

BX   = version number (see Note)

Note:

■ The major version number is returned in register BH, and the
minor version number is returned in register BL. For example, if
MSCDEX version 2.10 is loaded, the function will return 020AH in
register BX.

MSCDEX Function 0DH   [2.0]
Get CD-ROM Units

Returns a list of the systemwide logical drive identifiers that are
assigned to CD-ROM drives.

Call with:

AH   = 15H

AL   = 0DH

ES:BX   = segment:offset of buffer (see Notes)

Returns:

Nothing (information placed in buffer; see Notes)

Notes:

■ Upon return, the buffer contains a series of 1-byte entries. Each entry is a logical unit code assigned to a CD-ROM drive (0 = A, 1 = B, etc.); the units might not be consecutive.

■ The largest buffer that will ever be needed is 26 bytes. The actual size needed can be determined by calling MSCDEX Function 00H.

MSCDEX Function 0EH [2.0]
Get or Set Volume Descriptor Preference

Sets the CD-ROM Extensions to scan for the supplementary volume descriptor (SVD) rather than for the primary volume descriptor (PVD) on the specified drive, if an SVD is present. Can also be used to get the current preference setting for a particular CD-ROM drive.

Call with:

To get descriptor preference
AH   = 15H
AL   = 0EH
BX   = 0000H
CX   = drive (0 = A, 1 = B, etc.)

To set descriptor preference
AH   = 15H
AL   = 0EH
BX   = 0001H
CX   = drive (0 = A, 1 = B, etc.)
DH   = volume descriptor preference
         01H = primary volume descriptor (PVD)
         02H = supplementary volume descriptor (SVD)
DL   = supplementary volume descriptor preference
         00H if DH = 1
         01H if shift-Kanji (unregistered ISO character set)

Returns:

If function successful
Carry flag = clear

and, if called with BX = 0000H
DX   = preference settings (see above; 0000H = not supported
              by MSCDEX)

If function unsuccessful
Carry flag = set
AX   = error code

Note:

■ A CD-ROM drive set to scan for the SVD will use the PVD if no
SVD is present.

MSCDEX Function 0FH [2.0]
Get Directory Entry

Searches a CD-ROM directory for a specific path and filename and, if
a match is found, returns information about the corresponding file.

Call with:

AH   = 15H
AL   = 0FH
CX   = drive (0 = A, 1 = B, etc.)
ES:BX   = segment:offset of ASCIIZ pathname (cannot contain
              wildcard characters)
SI:DI   = segment:offset of 255-byte buffer to receive directory
              information

Returns:

If function successful
Carry flag = clear
AX   = format of CD-ROM volume
              00H if High Sierra
              01H if ISO-9660

and directory record placed in specified buffer

If function unsuccessful
Carry flag = set
AX   = error code

Notes:

■ The directory record format on High Sierra disks is as follows:

Offset	Length	Description
00H	1	length of directory entry (in bytes)
01H	1	length of XAR in LBN
02H	4	LBN of data, Intel byte order
06H	4	LBN of data, Motorola byte order
0AH	4	length of file, Intel byte order
0EH	4	length of data, Motorola byte order
12H	6	date and time
18H	1	file flags
19H	1	reserved
1AH	1	interleave size
1BH	1	interleave skip factor
1CH	2	volume set sequence number, Intel byte order
1EH	2	volume set sequence number, Motorola byte order
20H	1	length of name (n bytes)
21H	n	filename (n = 1–32)
21H+n	0 or 1	optional padding byte if n is odd
varies	varies	system-dependent data

■ The directory record format on ISO-9660 disks is as follows:

Offset	Length	Description
00H	1	length of directory entry (in bytes)
01H	1	length of XAR in LBN
02H	4	LBN of data, Intel byte order
06H	4	LBN of data, Motorola byte order
0AH	4	length of file, Intel byte order
0EH	4	length of data, Motorola byte order
12H	7	date and time
19H	1	file flags
1AH	1	interleave size
1BH	1	interleave skip factor
1CH	2	volume set sequence number, Intel byte order
1EH	2	volume set sequence number, Motorola byte order
20H	1	length of name (n bytes)
21H	n	filename (n = 1–32)
21H+n	0 or 1	optional padding byte if n is odd
varies	varies	system-dependent data

MSCDEX Function 10H [2.1]
Send Device Request

Provides a direct path of communication between an application and the device driver for a specific CD-ROM unit. This allows a program to obtain hardware-dependent information and to request operations that are not supported by MS-DOS or MSCDEX function calls.

Call with:

AH	= 15H
AL	= 10H
CX	= drive (0 = A, 1 = B, etc.)
ES:BX	= segment:offset of driver request header

Returns:

Nothing (driver status in request header)

Notes:

■ The driver request headers passed to this function are in the same format as the headers used by MSCDEX and MS-DOS to communicate with the CD-ROM device driver. Request headers have the following structure:

Offset	Length	Description
00H	1	length of request header (in bytes)
01H	1	unit (drive)
02H	1	command code
03H	2	status (returned by driver)
05H	8	reserved (0)
0DH	varies	command code–specific information

■ The command codes supported by CD-ROM drivers are as follows:

00H	Initialization
03H	I/O control (IOCTL) read
07H	Flush input buffers
0BH (11)	Flush output buffers #
0CH (12)	I/O control (IOCTL) write
0DH (13)	Device open
0EH (14)	Device close
80H (128)	Read long
82H (130)	Read long with prefetch
83H (131)	Seek

(continued)

84H (132)	Play *
85H (133)	Stop play *
86H (134)	Write long #
87H (135)	Write long with verify #

Command codes marked with * are supported only by extended CD-ROM drivers. Command codes marked with # are supported by CD-ROM authoring systems or by drivers for (as yet non-existent) writable CD-ROM devices.

■ If the driver encounters an error, it sets bit 15 of the status field and places a specific error code in bits 0–7 of the same field:

00H	Write-protect violation
01H	Unknown unit
02H	Drive not ready
03H	Unknown command
04H	CRC error
05H	Bad request header length
06H	Seek error
07H	Unknown media
08H	Sector not found
09H	Printer out of paper
0AH	Write fault
0BH	Read fault
0CH	General failure
0DH	Reserved
0EH	Reserved
0FH	Invalid disk change

■ The request header formats for each command code are documented in the Microsoft MS-DOS CD-ROM Extensions Hardware-Dependent Device Driver Specification, document number 000080010-100-O00-1186, dated August 8, 1988.

Other Titles from Microsoft Press

ADVANCED MS-DOS® PROGRAMMING, 2nd edition

Ray Duncan

"ADVANCED MS-DOS PROGRAMMING is one of the most authoritative in its field…"   **PC Magazine**

ADVANCED MS-DOS PROGRAMMING has been completely revised and expanded to include MS-DOS version 4.0, DOS and OS/2 compatibility, and the new PS/2 ROM BIOS services. Ray Duncan begins his instructive guide to assembly-language and C programming in the PC/MS-DOS environment by giving you an overview on the structure and loading of MS-DOS. He addresses key programming topics, including character devices, mass storage, memory management, and process management. You will find a detailed reference section of system functions and interrupts for all current versions of MS-DOS; ROM BIOS information including the EGA, VGA, PC/AT, and PS/2; version 4.0 of the Lotus/Intel/ Microsoft Expanded Memory Specification; and advice on writing "well-behaved" *vs* hardware-dependent applications. The examples, ranging from programming samples to full-length utilities, are instructive and extremely utilitarian and were developed using the Microsoft Macro Assembler version 5.1 and Microsoft C Compiler version 5.1.

688 pages, softcover, $24.95   Order Code 86-96668

THE MS-DOS® ENCYCLOPEDIA

Foreword by Bill Gates

"…for those with any technical involvement in the PC industry, this is the one and only volume worth reading."   **PC WEEK**

If you're a serious MS-DOS programmer, this is the ultimate reference. The MS-DOS ENCYCLOPEDIA is an unmatched sourcebook for version-specific technical data, including annotations of more than 100 system function calls—each accompanied by C-callable, assembly language routines; for comprehensive version-specific descriptions and usage information on each of the 90 user commands— the most comprehensive ever assembled; and for documentation of a host of key programming utilities. Articles cover debugging, TSRs, installable device drivers, writing applications for upward compatibility, and much, much more. The MS-DOS ENCYCLOPEDIA contains hundreds of hands-on examples, thousands of lines of code, plus an index to commands and topics. Covering MS-DOS through version 3.2, with a special section on version 3.3, this encyclopedia is the preeminent, most authoritative reference for every professional MS-DOS programmer.

1600 pages, 7³/₄ x 10, hardcover, $134.95   **Order Code 86-96122**
                              softcover, $69.95   **Order Code 86-96833**

MICROSOFT® MOUSE PROGRAMMER'S REFERENCE
Microsoft Press

Currently attached to more than one million personal computers, the Microsoft Mouse is one of the world's most popular PC peripherals and an industry standard. No software program—custom or commercial—is complete without support for the Microsoft Mouse. This guide—by a team of experts from the Hardware Division of Microsoft Corporation—enables intermediate- to advanced-level programmers to add mouse support to their programs, thus adding value and ease of use. It's both an essential reference to the mouse programming interface and a handbook for writing functional mouse menus. The two 5.25-inch companion disks include:

- MOUSE.LIB and EGA.LIB
- mouse menus
- a collection of valuable programs in BASIC, QuickBASIC, QuickC, Microsoft C, Pascal, Microsoft Macro Assembler, and FORTRAN

The MICROSOFT MOUSE PROGRAMMER'S REFERENCE is the most authoritative and value-packed reference guide available.

336 pages, softcover with two 5.25-inch disks, $29.95
Order Code 86-97005

ADVANCED OS/2 PROGRAMMING
Ray Duncan

Here is the most complete and accurate source of information on the new features and structure of OS/2 for C and assembly-language programmers. Topics include: porting existing MS-DOS applications to OS/2, programming in both real and protected modes, writing true multitasking programs, and more. ADVANCED OS/2 PROGRAMMING contains an example-packed reference section on the more than 250 OS/2 1.1 kernel functions, with complete information on their calling arguments, return values, and special uses. ADVANCED OS/2 PROGRAMMING will improve your capability as an OS/2 programmer.

800 pages, softcover, $24.95   **Order Code 86-96106**

INSIDE OS/2

Gordon Letwin, Chief Architect, Systems Software, Microsoft
Foreword by Bill Gates

"Mere recommendations aren't good enough for INSIDE OS/2…. If you're at all serious about OS/2 you must buy this book."

Dr. Dobb's Journal

INSIDE OS/2 is an unprecedented, candid, and exciting technical examination of OS/2. Letwin takes you inside the philosophy, key development issues, programming implications, and future of OS/2. He also provides the first in-depth look at each of OS/2's design elements, how they work alone, and their roles in the system. A valuable and revealing programmer-to-programmer discussion of the graphical user interface, multitasking, memory management, protection, encapsulation, interprocess communication, direct device access, and more. You can't get a more inside view. This is a book no OS/2 programmer can afford to be without!

304 pages, softcover, $19.95   Order Code 86-96288

MICROSOFT QUICKC® PROGRAMMING
The Microsoft® Guide to Using the QuickC® Compiler

The Waite Group: Mitchell Waite, Stephen Prata, Bryan Costales, and Harry Henderson

MICROSOFT QUICKC PROGRAMMING is the most authoritative introduction to every significant element of Microsoft QuickC available today! A detailed overview of the language elements gets you started. And the scores of programming examples and tips show you how to manipulate QuickC's variable types, decision structures, functions, and pointers; how to program using the Graphics Library; how to port Pascal to QuickC; how to interface your QuickC programs with assembly language; how to use the powerful source-level debugger; and more. If you're new to C or familiar with Microsoft QuickBASIC or Pascal, MICROSOFT QUICKC PROGRAMMING is for you. If you're a seasoned programmer, you'll find solid, reliable information that's available nowhere else.

608 pages, softcover, $19.95   Order Code 86-96114

THE 80386 BOOK
Assembly Language Programmer's Guide for the 80386

Ross P. Nelson

If you are an experienced 8088/8086 user, this is the most comprehensive and authoritative introduction to the 80386 chip you'll find. Nelson gives you a detailed analysis of the CPU, memory architecture, the protection scheme, compatibility with 8086/80286 chips, and much more. You will gain good 80386 assembly-language programming techniques through the scores of programming and design examples included in this book. A complete instruction set reference and information-packed appendixes makes THE 80386 BOOK a valuable reference tool.

464 pages, softcover, $24.95   Order Code 86-96494

PROGRAMMING WINDOWS
The Microsoft Guide to Programming for the MS-DOS Presentation Manager
Charles Petzold

PROGRAMMING WINDOWS is the first full technical discussion of Windows and your fastest route to great Windows applications. Special topics cover memory management, fonts, dynamically linkable libraries, manipulating the resources of the graphics device interface, and much more. Included are scores of valuable sample programs and utilities. Even if you have little programming experience you will gain a solid understanding of Windows' dynamics and its relationship to MS-DOS and the IBM PC.

864 pages, softcover, $24.95   Order Code 86-96130
hardcover, $34.95   Order Code 86-96189

THE PROGRAMMER'S PC® SOURCEBOOK
Reference Tables for the IBM PC®s and Compatibles, PS/2® Machines, and DOS®
Thom Hogan

At last! A reference book to save you the frustration of searching high and low for key pieces of technical data. Here is important factual information from hundreds of sources that have been culled and integrated into convenient, accessible charts, tables, and listings. It's the first place to turn for immediate, accurate information about your computer and its operating system. It's all here. THE PROGRAMMER'S PC SOURCEBOOK covers all versions of PC-DOS and MS-DOS, and all IBM computers, including the PS/2 series. Among the charts included are DOS commands and utilities; interrupts; mouse information; and EMS support; ROM BIOS calls and supporting tables; memory layout, interrupt vectors; RAM parameters; keyboard-related charts; extended character set; and more.

560 pages, softcover, $24.95   Order Code 86-96296

PROGRAMMER'S GUIDE TO PC® & PS/2™ VIDEO SYSTEMS
Maximum Video Performance From the EGA, VGA, HGC, and MCGA

Richard Wilton

Do you want maximum video performace from your EGA, VGA, HGC, or MCGA graphics adapter? The PROGRAMMER'S GUIDE TO PC & PS/2 VIDEO SYSTEMS shows you how. No other book offers such detailed, specialized programming data, techniques, and advice to help you tackle the exacting problems of programming directly to the video hardware. And no other book offers the more than 100 invaluable source code examples included here. Whatever graphics output you want—text, circles, region fill, bit blocks, or animation, you'll do it faster and more effectively with PROGRAMMER'S GUIDE TO PC & PS/2 VIDEO SYSTEMS—a one-of-a-kind resource for every serious programmer.

544 pages, softcover, $24.95   Order Code 86-96163

PROGRAMMER'S QUICK REFERENCE SERIES

MS-DOS® FUNCTIONS

Ray Duncan

This great quick reference is full of the kind of information every programmer—professional or casual—needs right at his fingertips. You'll find data—all clearly organized—on each MS-DOS system service call (accessed via Interrupts 20H through 2FH) along with a list of the parameters it requires, the results it returns, version dependencies, and valuable programming notes. Covering MS-DOS through version 3.3.

128 pages, 4³/₄ x 8, softcover, $5.95   Order Code 86-96411

IBM® ROM BIOS

Ray Duncan

If you're an assembly-language, Pascal, or C programmer—no matter what your experience level—this is an incredibly useful reference. IBM ROM BIOS: PROGRAMMER'S QUICK REFERENCE is a handy and compact guide to the ROM BIOS services of IBM PC, PC/AT and PS/2 machines. Designed for quick and easy access to information, this guide gives you all the core information on each ROM BIOS service: its required parameters and returned results, version dependencies, and some valuable programming notes. Keep this within easy reach!

128 pages, 4³/₄ x 8, softcover, $5.95   Order Code 86-96478

Microsoft Press books are available wherever fine books are sold, or credit card orders can be placed by calling **1-800-638-3030** *(in Maryland call collect 824-7300).*

The manuscript for this book was prepared and submitted to Microsoft Press in electronic form. Text files were processed and formatted using Microsoft Word.

Cover design by Thomas A. Draper
Interior text design by Greg Hickman
Principal typography by Rodney Cook
Color separations by Wescan Color Corporation

Text composition by Microsoft Press in Times Roman with display in Times Roman Bold, using the Magna composition system and the Linotronic 300 laser imagesetter.